In Search of
Nathaniel Woodard

Victorian Founder of Schools

MEMENTO
D̄NE
NATHANIEL
WOODARD
HVJ 'COLL'
FVNDATORIS

NATHANIEL WOODARD
FOVNDER AND FIRST PROVOST
BORN MARCH 21ST 1810, DIED APRIL 25TH 1891.

Nathaniel Woodard (1811-91). Painted after his death by Charles Goldsborough Anderson (1865-1936) from a photograph taken in 1870, it hangs now in the Dining Hall at Lancing College. His year of birth is recorded as 1810, a mistake repeated at his Vault.

IN SEARCH OF
NATHANIEL WOODARD

Victorian Founder of Schools

David Gibbs

PHILLIMORE

2011

Published by
PHILLIMORE & CO. LTD
Andover, Hampshire, England
www.phillimore.co.uk

ISBN 978-1-86077-667-0

Printed and bound in Malta
Manufactured by Jellyfish Print Solutions Ltd

Contents

List of Illustrations

Frontispiece: Portrait of Nathaniel Woodard

Illustration Acknowledgements

My grateful thanks to: the Council of Lancing College for allowing the frontispiece and number 14 to be reproduced; Matthew Gibbs, who took numbers 2, 5-10, 16, 24, 26-8; Elisabeth Lewis-Jones and Ben Carrett of Liquid PR who act for the Woodard Corporation and provided numbers 1, 11-13, 15, 17-21, 29; the individual schools provided numbers 22-3, 25, 30-2 and all those in the Appendix; and number 4 was provided by the author.

Acknowledgements

The date 21 March 2011 is the 200th anniversary of the birth of Nathaniel Woodard, priest and founder of schools. When he died in 1891 there were 10 members of this High Church Anglican family of schools: today 45 belong. Bridging the gap between the state and the private sectors, the Woodard schools are a significant part of the national educational landscape.

Woodard was a remarkable man who accomplished great things, yet today as an historical figure is largely unknown. I have set out to follow his footsteps, make sense of his life and achievement, and put them into context. Three books have been written about him, the last more than 40 years ago. Sir John Otter, his son-in-law, wrote a slightly sanitised biography, *Nathaniel Woodard – A Memoir of His Life* (Bodley Head) 1925; Kenneth Kirk, Bishop of Oxford, and Provost of the Woodard Corporation, outlined the background to the schools in, *The Story of the Woodard Schools* (Abbey Press) 1952; the Canadian historian Brian Heeney wrote a scholarly account of their creation and development up to the time of his death, *Mission to the Middle Classes – The Woodard Schools 1848-1891* (SPCK) 1969.

Histories of Woodard's first three schools, all in Sussex, have captured the excitement of their birth and subsequent, not always straightforward, growth and development: Basil Handford, *Lancing College – History and Memoirs* (Phillimore) 1986; Jeremy Tomlinson, *Lancing College A Portrait* (Lancing College) 1998; Peter King, *Hurstpierpoint College – The School by the Downs 1849-1995* (Phillimore) 1997; and my own, *A School with a View – A History of Ardingly College 1858-2008* (James & James) 2008. In addition Garth Pedler, *A Prep School in Somerset – The Story of the Junior School of King's College, Taunton to 1982* (Gresham Books) 2007 has provided a fund of information about the Woodard world, and C.H. Murphy's, *Scenes from a Century – Worksop College 1895-1995* (Worksop College), 1995 is an evocative pictorial record.

Many people have helped and accompanied me on this journey of discovery, not least in reading the first draft. They include three current Woodard heads, Jonathan Gillespie (Lancing), Tim Manly (Hurstpierpoint) and Brendan Wignall (Ellesmere) who in the midst of their immensely busy lives found the time to advise perceptively from the inside; archivists Andrea King (Ardingly), Anne Drewery (Lancing), Janet Pennington (ex-Lancing and also author of the Woodard entry in the DNB), Martin Williams (Hurstpierpoint) and Jane Collard (Worksop) were unfailingly helpful in advising me and also steering me towards relevant material; the registrar of Lancing, Jeremy Tomlinson, shared with me his great knowledge of the world of his school; two recently retired and highly experienced HMC heads, Tom Wheare and Giles Mercer, provided a wide and insightful perspective; and Joe Fyles, sometime head of history at Chigwell School, navigated me knowledgeably through the highways and byways of the Victorian church. Without exception their comments were pertinent and opened up many new lines of enquiry. I learned a lot from them all.

I am most grateful to Neil Lyon who let me see the unpublished manuscript of his authoritative, *The Public Schools – A History of Boys Independent Schools in England*.

At the Woodard Corporation, Canon Brendan Clover, Senior Provost, has helped to steer the project throughout and has written the Foreword. Chris Wright, former head of a Woodard school and now Director of Education, has been a thoughtful adviser on the contemporary Woodard world; and Jill Shorthose, Office Manager, a thoroughly helpful link with the individual schools.

My son, architectural student Matthew Gibbs, accompanied me on several visits of exploration, took a number of the photographs and reminded me just how valuable are Pevsner's Architectural *Guides to the Buildings of England*. Philippa, my wife, has not only tolerated uncomplainingly the constant presence of Nathaniel Woodard in our home but also read the manuscript and made many helpful suggestions.

I have enjoyed working with the Phillimore team of Sarah Pavey, Production Editor, Andrew Illes, Business Manager, and Noel Osborne, Chairman, and appreciated greatly their professionalism and skill.

It goes without saying that all errors of fact and judgement are mine alone.

Foreword

By any reckoning Nathaniel Woodard was a giant in the land. His concern to educate the young and to nurture them in the truth of the Christian gospel was at the heart of a project whose aim was nothing less than the transformation of contemporary society. Education was a means of rescuing that society from its ills. Nathaniel Woodard's contribution to the educational movement of Victorian society was, arguably, the most significant of any single individual. And yet he remains in Church and State relatively unknown.

This retelling of his story is part of an attempt to bring due honour to his name and to celebrate his achievements as the 200th Anniversary of his birth comes around. Here was a man of steely determination, whose 'one idea' lead to the establishment of a group of schools and of an educational purpose which still, under God, may have the potential to 'promote and extend Christian education' (the Charitable Object of the Corporation) in line with the doctrines and principles of the Church of England and the Church in Wales, and to help in the transformation of contemporary society.

Today, the Woodard schools is a fascinating group of independent and maintained sector schools seeking to offer a holistic education which places the needs of the child at the centre of a value rich and value driven education, where good practice is shared and developed, in a context in which the truths of the Christian faith are proclaimed as much as diversity is celebrated. Woodard schools are ideally placed in the current educational landscape to pursue the ambitions of the founder today by playing a lead role in meeting the needs of communities, and in the delivery of first class education.

Canon Brendan Clover
Senior Provost

ONE

Introduction

Nathaniel Woodard was born on 21 March 1811. For a man who was to develop a devout sense of mission, blessed with energy and drive, and granted 80 years of life, 1811 was a good year in which to be born. Britain was on the move. During his lifetime the population was to increase from 12 million in 1811 to 33 million in 1891. The Industrial Revolution was transforming an agricultural economy and rural society into an industrial and urban country. Railways and steam ships expanded horizons and also made possible an empire. It was an age of reform, not only politically but also of institutions. This immense growth, accompanied by radical change, was to form the backcloth of Nathaniel Woodard's life and work.

The great Victorians – Brunel, Livingstone, Florence Nightingale, Gladstone, Disraeli, Darwin, W.G. Grace, Dickens, for example – possessed not only energy, drive and a sense of mission, but also, and crucially, confidence and an unquestioned belief in their own role and destiny. They built and what they built survived.

Woodard was all of these things but he was also personally unassuming, eschewed the public limelight and would not even allow his portrait to be painted. In any event education, which was to be his life's work, is rarely an arena in which fame or fortunes are made. Religion was his driving force. The aim of his life was to restore to the heart of the nation what he regarded as the true faith, the Church of England shaped by its Catholic heritage; and he determined to do this by means of filling a profound gap in the provision of education.

One by-product of industrialising, manufacturing, urbanizing Britain was its growing middle classes and these were to play a key role in the transformation of the country. The lawyers, doctors, teachers, farmers, engineers, tradesmen, shopkeepers, clerks and administrators, and colonial district officers became the backbone of a modern industrial society. They had aspirations.

1   *Concert in the Hurstpierpoint College quad. Church, school, music and Gothic architecture were to be at the heart of Woodard's vision and life's work.*

Woodard recognised that the educational system as a whole failed to provide for the sons of the bulk of these middle classes. The 'ancient' public schools provided for the upper classes. New foundations such as Cheltenham, Marlborough and Radley catered for the upper and more affluent end of the middle classes, the sons of clergymen, army officers and colonial civil servants. Unable to afford these schools, the lower and less affluent middle classes regarded the parochial schools as limited, and the classical curriculum of the moribund grammar schools as irrelevant to their needs. Here was Woodard's opportunity. Dedicated to placing the Established Church at the heart of national life, he saw low cost middle class education as the means by which the Church of England could counteract both the expanding role of the State and the growing influence of the Nonconformists.

He cannot really be described as an educationalist, and certainly he developed no profound philosophy of education. What he did do, however, was to establish an Anglican teaching order, and as well to found and build five schools – Lancing, Hurstpierpoint and Ardingly in Sussex, Denstone and Ellesmere in the Midlands. He took over and revitalised the school which became King's College, Taunton, secured the foundation of St Cuthbert's, later Worksop, and incorporated three girls schools – St Michael's, Bognor, St Anne's, Abbots Bromley, and SS Mary and John, Lichfield. Collectively he welded together these 10 schools into the Society of St Nicolas, the overarching charitable organisation which became the focal point of his family of schools.

St Nicolas, incidentally, was the long-serving Bishop of Myra in Asia Minor in the early part of the fourth century. The Patron Saint of Children, he is, of course, universally known to them today in his disguise as 'Santa Claus'. In the Middle Ages four hundred churches in England alone were dedicated to his honour. His resolution and profound faith in the face of persecution created a striking and protective image for Woodard's schools. He has, too, been immortalised by Benjamin Britten in his choral work 'Saint Nicolas', commissioned for the Centenary Celebrations of Lancing College in 1948, and sung first by the combined choirs of Lancing, Hurstpierpoint, Ardingly and St Michael's (by then at Petworth), conducted by the composer.

Today the Woodard Corporation, as the Society is known, is composed of 45 schools, 22 owned, 15 affiliated, eight associated, educating more than 30,000 pupils, taught by 3,000 teachers. All of them are Church of England faith schools.

We need to note, however, the very different environment of Woodard's England. Christianity was still interwoven in the lives of people of all classes and informed public discourse and institutions of learning. Today, Christianity has increasingly found itself on the margins of much of national life in a society which has a multi-faith dimension. The concept of faith schools arouses explicit and vocal opposition from some quarters at local and national levels. A generally supportive atmosphere can no longer be taken for granted. The challenge facing the Woodard and other Christian schools today is, therefore, sharper and more fundamental than in the 19th century.

The Woodard schools are a familiar feature of the English educational landscape but who was Nathaniel Woodard? Where did he come from? What shaped his outlook? How and where did he operate? What sort of a person was he? And, crucially, what is his relevance today?

This journey sets out to find answers to these questions. It starts in his birthplace now buried amidst a 1950s housing estate in Basildon New Town in Essex. It visits remote vicarages in Norfolk and Essex, an Oxford college, Bethnal Green in London's East End, the bustling port town of Shoreham, a substantial town house in the Sussex village of Henfield, Manchester Cathedral, a vault in the magnificent Lancing College Chapel, high on the South Downs not far from Brighton, together with some of the most beautifully located schools in the land. It finishes with four new Woodard Academy schools currently being built in Littlehampton and Lancing village in Sussex, and planned in Maidstone, Kent and Stoke-on-Trent. They are beacons of hope for the future of young people.

Two

A Man of Essex

Nathaniel Woodard was born at Basildon Hall in south-east Essex, close to the Thames estuary. He was the ninth of the 12 children of John and Mary (née Sillery) Woodard.

The Woodards were a family of the lesser gentry, the sort of people about whom Jane Austen wrote so memorably at this time. Woodards can be traced back to the 17th century in this area, and some of them were clergymen. John Woodard, though, had been brought up in Reading, and his wife came from Southampton. She was an only child and had some of the financial resources necessary to acquire Basildon Hall.

This was an agricultural life. Basildon then was no more than a hamlet based around the Hall, whose lands ran down to the marshes of the Thames. Farming was not easy in Nathaniel's childhood. The economy, and with it the price of grain, had flourished during the Napoleonic Wars, but their cessation following the battle of Waterloo in 1815 led to a period of falling prices and surplus labour, exacerbated by the return of veterans from the Wars. Add to this the increasing mechanisation of agriculture and a series of poor harvests, and the result was agricultural distress accompanied by high unemployment. In 1830, just when Nathaniel might have wanted his father's financial support for university, the Captain Swing Riots broke out throughout south-east England. Rick burning and machine breaking were rife, especially in Essex, and £3,000 (approximately £200,000 in today's values) worth of damage was done to the family farm.

Not unusually for those times, Nathaniel Woodard received no formal education or schooling. His parents could not afford one of the public schools such as Eton, Winchester or Westminster. The local elementary schools run by the parish were considered for the poor only, and the endowed Tudor and Stuart grammar schools (Brentwood, Chigwell and Felsted were the nearest) were seen, for the most part, as moribund, offering only a traditional classical education. His mother, Mary, would have done what she could at home, teaching him to read and write, but with 11 other children, and a busy farmhouse to run, her time and attention were limited.

The practical life of the farm which so absorbed his father and elder brothers held little attraction for Nathaniel. He was sensitive, devout and musical, all of these inculcated by his mother. Many years later he wrote: 'When I was a boy, I knew the organ lofts of half the best churches in London.' This is a curious statement. Is it to suggest that a young boy was wandering around London on his own? Or was he staying with a relative, taking the opportunity to escape from the restrictive society of a remote and rural Essex community? In fact the coach journey from home would have taken only three to four hours. What it does suggest is that church music, which he was to love all his life, took early root, and likewise the spirit of enterprise and adventure.

He was an individualist and a distinctive personality. His contemporaries in later life commented on his great sense of fun. He was a conversationalist who

2   *The site of Basildon Hall in 2011. Here Woodard was born and brought up. Then a substantial farm with land extending down to the Thames, it was demolished in the 1950s to make way for the building of Basildon New Town. Two hundred years after his birth in 1811, all that remains is the site of its moat and the mound on the right of the photo on which the Hall was built.*

loved banter and puns, and he had an uproarious sense of humour and a terse wit. All of these will have been forged in that secure but what must have been slightly chaotic household on the high ground, looking down to the marshes of the Thames estuary and beyond to the hills of Kent.

His mother was a devout Anglican and brought up her children to say their prayers, and know their Bible; and the family worshipped at the local parish church in the hamlet of Laindon. After he died, there was found stowed away in a box, amongst his possessions, some of his earliest writings, including a document named Covenant and dated 20 November 1830 (when he was 19): 'I desire humbly to enter covenant with Thee this day … I have been too much given up to the foolish things of this world and often, O Lord, as Thou knowest I have smarted for my love of the things of sense … I will by Thy help henceforth follow Thee whithersoever Thou goest, whether it be in plenty or adversity ….'

Many years later in, 1888, he wrote to Edward Lowe, one of his chief lieutenants: 'I have sworn and am steadfastly purposed to give my life and every farthing I possess to the work and from this I cannot turn aside, so that mine for forty years has not been a voluntary act.' It was clear that he believed strongly that he had a divine mission. He was, too, a driven man who regarded obstacles as both challenges to be overcome and opportunities. There was one means only by which he could go about God's work and that was through ordination into the priesthood of the Church of England. But this required a university degree and for that he needed at least some formal academic training, apart, obviously, from the financial support necessary for the years of study. His appeal, through the contact of a friend, to the Bishop of Bath and Wells for ordination without a degree failed.

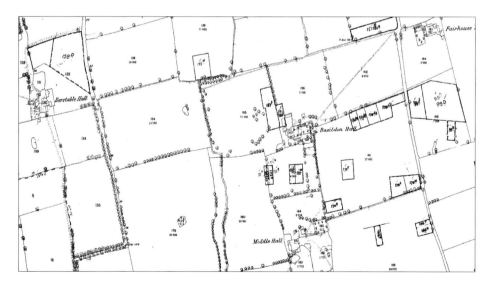

3   *Basildon Hall in the OS map of 1880.*

4   *The original Leicester School at Hatfield Broad Oak in 2011. Now converted into a private home, this was built by the Reverend Leicester in the 1820s for the poor children in the parish. It was here that Woodard gained his first experience in teaching and found the inspiration for his life's work.*

And so, in preparation for university entrance, he received some tutoring from the Reverend William Stratton, the rector of Boughton, a village not far from Downham Market in west Norfolk. Then in 1832 he was appointed resident tutor to the four sons of the Reverend George Leicester, curate at Hatfield Broad Oak, close to Bishop's Stortford, and in return Leicester agreed to help him prepare for university entrance. Leicester was a distinguished academic who had been Senior Wrangler at Cambridge in 1815.

These two years in the vicarage at Hatfield Broad Oak were to be a formative influence in his life. Not only was he given sufficient academic grounding to cope with an Oxford degree course, but also he was given the opportunity to teach the village children at the school which the curate had established and built. The first seed of his educational mission had been sown. In addition, his religious philosophy was beginning to take shape. Leicester believed strongly in the dictates of the 1662 Prayer Book which, amongst other things, made possible the practice of confession.

Woodard's luck was turning because also at this time, fortuitously, two aunts who recognised his promise and ambition provided him with enough money to go to university to read for a degree. He was on his way. But before he left his home environment in Essex for good, he acquired one further influence from these parts – a wife. For several years he had courted Elizabeth (always known as Eliza) Harriet Brill, and although it was rare for an undergraduate to be married, they were wed on 24 March 1836 and set up home at Great Parndon, now overwhelmed by Harlow New Town.

THREE

The Oxford Movement

Cambridge was the obvious university for an Essex man in the pre-railway age, particularly having been tutored by a distinguished Cambridge Mathematics graduate, but in fact there were stirrings in Oxford which attracted Woodard. The summer of 1833 had witnessed the sermon in the University Church by the Reverend John Keble of Oriel College (published as *National Apostasy*) and then the publication of the first *Tracts for the Times* whereby Keble and his followers became known as Tractarians. The Oxford Movement had been launched.

Profoundly influencing Woodard, it was to colour and shape both his religious philosophy and his life's work. John Henry Newman, John Keble and Edward Pusey, priests in the Church of England and Fellows of Oriel, were to emerge as its key figures, and it was at its peak between 1833 and 1845. Concerned by the loss of the fire and spirit of the Church in its earliest days, they were dismayed by the tone of the Church of England in which too many of its clergy had come to epitomise characters who were later to appear in Trollope's novels, excessively worldly, complacent, comfortable and unambitious. The Tractarians sought to renew the Anglican Church by restoring its Catholic heritage. With Newman as the driving intellectual force, they set out to lead a second Reformation, inculcating a spiritual revival which was strong in faith, devout, reverent in worship and based firmly on the sacraments.

There were several features which were to recur in Woodard's subsequent work. The Oxford Movement rejected the Protestant element in Anglicanism in favour of the Catholic as it existed before the Reformation and notably denied the rights of Parliament to oversee the affairs of the Church. It paid very particular attention to the specific words of the Prayer Book in regard to confession which, as we shall see, was later to create substantial difficulties for Woodard; and from it stemmed the High Church ethos, culture and spirit, with its characteristic Gothic buildings, beauty of worship, and plainsong music.

Initially Woodard had hoped to study at Brasenose College, but in the event his impending marriage ruled that out; hence he went to Magdalen Hall, an institution with a long-standing Puritan tradition and located in the buildings which in due course became Hertford College.

In fact it took Woodard six years, instead of the usual three, to take a pass degree. He shared his time between undergraduate life at Oxford and his wife, Eliza, and three children, one of whom died as an infant, at Great Parndon.

Although by nature shy, Woodard was energetic socially and nothing if not tenacious. He made connections in this High Church world. Its ethos seeped into his soul and being, and in due course was to be firmly planted in his schools. He was in fact to devote his life to putting this particular theology into practice. Applying it to education and especially the education of the children of the middle classes was his vocation. Truly he was a great missionary of what became known as Anglo-Catholicism.

FOUR

London's East End

On 6 June 1841 Nathaniel Woodard was ordained deacon by Bishop Blomfield of London and given sole charge of St Bartholomew's, Bethnal Green, one of the poorest districts in early Victorian London. The silk-weaving industry which had once spread out from Spitalfields was now in decline. There were furniture, clothing, boot and shoe manufacturers crowded into narrow courts and streets. It was hugely over-crowded which was not surprising given that the population had risen from 33,000 in 1811 to 74,000 in 1841, and there had been outbreaks of cholera. Extreme poverty was endemic and its evidence loomed large in the reports of early reformers such as Edwin Chadwick and Southwood Smith in the 1840s.

Woodard threw himself into the work of the parish. He saw himself as the father of his flock, sharing with them in their joys and sadnesses, following the model of John Henry Newman in his work as a priest in St Clement's, Oxford. After a long wait he had finally launched his life's work. The church building was completed and he founded a school. Although given sole charge of the parish on a salary of £80 per annum, it was his understanding with the Bishop, and expectation, that he would be appointed vicar with its permanent rights, including a salary of £300 p.a., when the church was consecrated and the district given the status of an ecclesiastical parish.

This was his first direct experience of urban life and he was appalled by the godlessness, ignorance, and low moral and spiritual state, not only amongst those who were the working class, but also amongst those who were the employers, which in his parish were often the craftsmen in the workshops.

In June 1843 he spoke in a sermon on the confession of sins and the authority of the priest to absolve a penitent, quoting the Prayer Book: 'If there be any of you who by this means cannot quiet his own conscience herein, but requireth further comfort or counsel, let him come to me or to some other discreet and learned Minister of God's word and open his grief; that by the Ministry of God's Holy Word he may receive the benefit of absolution and ghostly counsel and advice.' A belief in confession and absolution smacked of popery and predictably aroused fear, and suspicion of Catholic leanings. There was a complaint to the Bishop who asked to see the text of the sermon. He wrote to Woodard: 'I cannot possibly appoint to any of the churches in Bethnal Green a person holding the opinions which you have embodied in that discourse ... I consider your sermon on confession and absolution to be erroneous on point of doctrine and highly dangerous as to the effects which it is likely to produce upon poor uneducated people. I give you full credit for devotedness and zeal and am deeply concerned that you should have adopted opinions and notions which are likely to mar the good effects of your many excellent qualities.'

There followed seven months of correspondence between the two. Woodard did not help his own cause by his obduracy and attention to the letter of the law rather than the broad principles which he was trying to espouse. He was young, inexperienced, perhaps misguided, and unwilling or unable to see the wider picture. The outcome was inevitable and Bishop Blomfield had no alternative but to dismiss him from his post.

It is important, however, that the wider context of this impasse is understood. Blomfield was a High Churchman who foresaw the divisiveness and distractions which would develop if Tractarian views were to spread to the London Diocese and in particular he feared an Evangelical backlash. He needed to be seen to be even-handed. He was also deeply committed to the immense task of parochial re-organisation, transferring resources from the more established and prosperous areas to the new inner cities, and in particular building new churches and schools in East London. He was very displeased to be diverted from this work by a 32-year-old priest-in-charge aping Newman and advocating confession and absolution and thereby stirring up unnecessary divisions in arguably the worst slum in England. Simply, he had more important matters to deal with.

Interestingly, and tellingly, several years later, Bishop Blomfield made a substantial donation to the Society of St Nicolas which Woodard had founded and also invited him to establish schools in his diocese. No one underestimated Woodard's abilities or the fundamental importance of his work. However, his unyielding doctrinal views and lack of tact and political *nous* were to create problems for him throughout his life, as we shall see.

The Bishop did find him another post as a curate at St James, Clapton in the neighbouring parish of Hackney but Woodard was bitterly disappointed. He had thrown himself into the work of the parish and he was clearly liked and appreciated by his parishioners. He was, however, out of tune with the prevailing theological ethos in the diocese.

By good fortune and no little skill in the use of connections, his friends, notably the Reverend Christie Miller of Harlow, found him a more congenial parish, some way from London on the Sussex coast.

Although dispirited, Woodard had actually accomplished much in his five years in the East End of London. He had learned about parish life, about the ways in which the local economy and society worked, and, of beneficial long-term

5   *Once St Bartholomew's, Bethnal Green. Part of the plan to build churches in the midst of the new inner cities, Woodard oversaw its construction (1843-45 by William Railton) whilst priest-in-charge. Gutted during the Blitz and then restored, it was converted into flats in the 1990s, 'quite tactfully', says Pevsner.*

consequence, he had attracted the attention of, and made links with, several leading philanthropists with interests in trying to shape this world. Notable amongst them were Henry Tritton, a partner in the bankers *Barclay, Bevan* and *Tritton*; A.J.B. Beresford-Hope, MP, builder of All Saints, Margaret Street and also brother-in-law of Lord Salisbury; Judge John Patteson; William Cotton, a former Governor of the Bank of England, who also supported school building in the East End; the High Church architect Richard Carpenter; and Joshua Watson, an important figure in the National Society, promoting Anglican elementary schools. These men were all devout and high minded Christians with a commitment to using their opportunities and resources amongst the poorest of the East End and elsewhere. In turn they admired the work of this diffident and awkward but very determined priest.

FIVE

Shoreham: The Design of a Teaching Order

Woodard's appointment as curate at Shoreham was a huge relief to him and his family. The parish was far more in tune with his theological outlook, there was a vicarage and stipend and the opportunity of a fresh start. It must also be said that it was an astute move by the Church of England to get this forceful but turbulent priest out of the way and out of sight.

Six miles west of Brighton, and four miles east of Worthing, both of them rapidly growing coastal towns without ports, Shoreham with a population of 4,000, was a harbour town at the mouth of the river Adur which had carved for itself a spectacular gap through the South Downs. Magdalen College, Oxford, with its sound High Church credentials, was the patron of its two churches. Woodard was put in charge of the church of St Mary de Haura (of the harbour), in what was known as New Shoreham, the busiest part of the parish, adjacent to the port. His parishioners were local tradesmen, clerks, a number of farmers and sea captains, most of them engaged in the business of the port; coal from the Tyne, timber, grain and other goods to and from the Baltic.

Woodard arrived in Shoreham at just the right time. The advent of the London Brighton & South Coast Railway in 1840 was the catalyst for bringing a small and inconsequential settlement into the orbit of the urban and industrial life of mid-Victorian Britain. He recognised the key role to be played in this transformation locally by the tradesmen classes who had influence over others in ships, shops, farms, businesses and workshops, and on a wider scale by the teachers, doctors, lawyers, engineers, clerks and administrators.

But the 1840s, the decade in which Woodard was launching his great work, was also a period of turbulence in society and politics. Overpopulation, high food prices, famine in Ireland, urban squalor and disease culminated in what became known

6   *St Mary de Haura, New Shoreham. As curate-in-charge of a bustling port church, this is where Woodard launched his life's work. In buildings overlooking the church green he sowed the seeds of the schools which became Lancing, Hurstpierpoint and Ardingly before transplanting them to their own buildings in virgin locations.*

as *The Hungry Forties*. Class divisions were exacerbated. This led to agitation that resulted in the repeal of the Corn Laws in 1846 and saw the Chartist movement rising to its peak with the immense Kennington Common demonstration of 1848. Though Britain characteristically avoided significant upheaval in this year, Europe was to know it simply as the Year of Revolutions. The Red Flag flew in Paris and Karl Marx and Friedrich Engels published their *Communist Manifesto*. It was Woodard's clear belief that these disconcerting events were the product of a secular society and, in particular, secular education.

He founded his first school for day boys, St Mary's, in January 1847 in his dining room in the Vicarage, employing an Oxford graduate to teach reading, writing and arithmetic, and offering as well land-surveying, navigation and book-keeping, addressing the needs of his local parishioners' sons. The fees were £3 p.a. with Latin and French as optional extras costing £1. Just over a year later on 1 August 1848 he opened next door Shoreham Grammar School and Collegiate Institution under the flag of the Society of St Mary and St Nicolas, which he had recently created. Boarders were charged £30 p.a. and the Reverend Henry Jacobs was its first headmaster.

Although it was an immediate success and pupil numbers rose rapidly, Jacobs soon fell out with Woodard.'... He misapprehended some of the principles of the Founder, especially that of the independent position of the Chaplain as guardian of the faith and morals of the boys', as explained by Sir John Otter in his 1925 biography of Woodard. Woodard was clear that, although the head was responsible for the academic life of the school, there would be a separately appointed chaplain responsible to himself. This dyarchy was to be a source of confusion and uncertainty. In fact the true reason for Jacob's departure may be more prosaic: 'He precipitately retreated from behind a door when he was found caressing the matron!', as the Reverend Edward Lowe, the first headmaster of Hurstpierpoint, later wrote to Professor Haverfield.

Importantly Woodard also persuaded Ashurst Turner Gilbert, Bishop of Chichester, to act as Visitor. The parish of Shoreham had what were known as Romish tendencies and the Bishop kept his distance, but his (not always uncritical) support and wise counsel were to be important to Woodard's grand design of building Anglican schools for the middle classes. The Bishop was clear in pointing out that the appearance, whatever the reality, of confession and absolution threatened the whole project. In 1853, for example, he refused to ordain a master into the priesthood: '... I have reason to believe that he will hear confessions and use absolution without regard to our Church's evident limitation of the practice.'

Shoreham was not the only local area of High Church support which was to benefit Woodard. At this time the Wagner family was making a significant impact in Brighton. The extremely wealthy and leading Anglo-Catholic, the Reverend Henry Wagner, was Vicar of Brighton, supported by his like-minded sons, Arthur and George, both priests, and they initiated, and often financed, the building of big Gothic churches in poor areas of Brighton, notably St Paul's, West Street (1848-49), St Michael and All Angels, Victoria Street (1858-61) and St Bartholomew's, Ann Street (1870-71). They reflected in their design and practice the revival of ritual in worship associated with the medieval Catholic church – long chancels with altars, sung services and vestments. The elder Richard Carpenter was the architect of St Paul's, and later his son, Richard Herbert (but always known as Herbert or Young Carpenter) added the upper tower which became a distinctive beacon in Brighton.

Arthur Wagner, the curate of St Paul's, was a major figure in this influential family and had pronounced views on ritual and ecclesiology which were influenced by his father-in-law, Joshua Watson, who as we have seen was a leading Tractarian and financial supporter of Woodard. These High Church features were viewed with suspicion by those who feared they were steps towards Roman Catholicism which they regarded as unEnglish and unnatural. There was significant opposition

7   *St Mary's House, New Shoreham. Now offices, the home from August 1848 of Woodard's first fully fledged boarding school, Shoreham Grammar School and Collegiate Institution.*

at St Paul's and in other local areas. The Anglo-Catholic movement was strong on the Sussex coast but also controversial.

In 1848 Woodard published what was to be his manifesto, *A Plea for the Middle Classes.* The aim was 'the provision of a good and complete education for the middle classes, at such a charge as will make it available for most of them.' But this was to be no ordinary education: 'It is my earnest wish and the object and intention of all the Benefactors, that for all future time the sons of any of Her then Majesty's subjects should be taught, together with sound grammar learning, the fear and honour of Almighty God, the Father, Son and the Holy Ghost, according to the doctrines of

8   *Blue plaque at St Mary's House on the church green. Shoreham Grammar School and Collegiate Institution in 1853 merged with the neighbouring St Mary's to form the College of St Mary and St Nicolas. This is turn moved to its new site on Lancing Hill in August 1857 and in due course became known as Lancing College.*

the Catholic Faith as is now set forth in the Book of the Offices and Administration of the Sacraments of the Church of England.' And soon afterwards, so as to have a vehicle to make it all happen, he founded *the Society of St Nicolas* (now known as the Woodard Corporation). It was to be governed by a Provost, who was Woodard himself from the outset, and 16 Fellows, and he divided the country into five areas or divisions. Essentially it was an Anglican missionary teaching order.

Woodard was a product of the Victorian age. He thought in terms of structures and systems, and he saw society in terms of class. It is not surprising, therefore, that his scheme for a national group of schools for the middle classes had three distinct grades or levels.

The Upper Middle schools were for the sons of gentlemen, officers, clergymen and superior trades people. The fees were to be £30 p.a. and it was hoped that these schools would provide both funds and teachers for the two lower grade schools. Shoreham Grammar School, founded as we have seen in 1848, was designated as the first upper middle school and was later known as Lancing College, having moved to its permanent home on Lancing Hill in 1857.

The Middle Middle schools were for the sons of tradesmen, farmers and superior clerks and charged 18 guineas. The first of this kind was opened as St John's at New Shoreham in 1849 and a year later transferred to temporary accommodation at the Mansion House in the village of Hurstpierpoint, in the lee of the South Downs to the north of Brighton, until its own buildings there were completed and ready for occupation in 1853.

The Lower Middle schools were for the sons of small shopkeepers, mechanics, clerks and others of limited means and charged fees of £15. It was expected that no parent would have an income greater than £100. The first of these Lower Middle schools was called St Saviour's School and was founded in 1858 in the New Shoreham buildings vacated by the school that became Lancing. It was transplanted to its permanent home at Ardingly in 1870.

The Upper Middle schools were to act as centres for groups of associated Middle Middle and Lower Middle schools with a provost residing at each centre. The plan was for a series of such groups, or *divisions* as they later became known, to be established throughout England.

9 & 10   *New Shoreham on the estuary of the river Adur. At the far left Lancing College with its chapel on the edge of the Downs, his first school, on the far right the tower of Woodard's church, St Mary de Haura, rising above the harbour community, where his grand designs began.*

There was, however, to be a ladder of opportunity, enabling the brightest boys to gain scholarships to move up from the Lower Middle to Middle and ultimately Upper Middle schools. Thus in our world of opportunity and inclusivity, there would exist the chance for a young boy of talent from a disadvantaged background to work his way up the ladder and then ultimately to Oxford or Cambridge.

To enable fees to be kept at such low levels, it was necessary to minimise costs. Teachers, the most important single component in any school, are expensive. Woodard wanted all his heads and most of his teachers to be in Holy Orders. Some came on very low stipends, seeing their vocation in doing God's work. Their support of the full High Anglican tradition was at least as important as their capacity to teach and this could lead to problems. For example, Sir John Otter wrote about the Reverend A.C. Wilson, Second Master at Lancing as follows: 'He had an enthusiastic admiration for the Founder, abounding love for the school, and deep concern for the spiritual welfare of the boys. He was generous to the fault of recklessness; rather uncertain and capricious in his conduct to the boys: a little fantastic in inventing new modes of punishment which would not now be tolerated. Everyone loved him in spite of his faults, and there was great sorrow when his extravagant expenditure brought his career at Lancing to an end.'

Woodard also established at Hurstpierpoint in 1853 what was in effect a training college for teachers, whereby *probationers* learned on the job, hoping to gain a teaching qualification by becoming what the Founder designated as an Associate of the Society of St Nicolas. Examinations were taken after three years training and teaching. It was an imaginative means of recruiting able, and cheap, teachers, derived perhaps from the lay brothers of the medieval monasteries; and the system flourished at Hurstpierpoint, Ardingly and Denstone until the end of the century. Today this concept is mirrored by the Woodard Corporation's very active involvement in training and continuous professional development of teachers, not least in the link being created between St Peter's Academy, Stoke-on-Trent and the education department of Manchester Metropolitan University.

Next in this teaching order were *monitors*, senior pupils who for a very low fee received some teaching and taught the younger pupils. The *monitorial* system was a device taken from schools in industrial towns wherein, by the provisions of the 1833 Factory Act, children employed in factories were to receive some, in practice usually sparse, teaching. Below the *monitors*, were *servitors*, who in return for a fee

of £5 p.a. worked as cleaners and kitchen assistants in the morning and received some basic tuition in the afternoon. They were similar in concept to the *sizars* at Cambridge University. Again it was an imaginative way of providing an education for boys from poor homes and keeping the schools' running costs to a minimum.

Woodard designed this network of schools for the middle classes as a means of supporting and developing the Church of England's work. They came to be characterised by the majestic chapels, Gothic architecture, plainsong music, and an emphasis on ceremony and ritual which were the distinguishing features of its Anglo-Catholic strand. As an overall scheme it was imaginative, clearly thought out and extremely ambitious.

His plans for education were not confined solely to schools. In 1850 he founded the Leyton Military and Engineering College on the edge of the East End of London, offering a technical and vocational training for the boys destined for the Royal Military College, Sandhurst, the Royal Military Academy, Woolwich, and the East India Company's College, Addiscombe. It was designed to provide a sound education in civil engineering. Its curriculum was practical and very modern: Surveying, Levelling and Hill-drawing; Fortification; French; Landscape drawing; and Hindustani and Hindi. As with his schools, there was a separate chaplain. It was not, however, cheap. There was an entry fee of two guineas, and fees were £60 p.a. but did not include tradesmen's bills, instruments and stationery. A private bedroom and sitting room cost five guineas. Fencing was an extra at £1 11s. 6d. Perhaps it was too expensive but the College never really became established and closed down in 1857.

It was not his only venture which was ahead of its time. His plans to create halls of residence for the products of his schools at Oxford and Cambridge at much cheaper rates than conventional college life had much to commend them but practicalities overruled. And at one stage he came close to purchasing the Agricultural College at Cirencester although it is not easy to see how this fitted into his overall scheme of things.

He was a man of many good ideas. Now it was necessary that at least some of them be made to happen.

Six

Sussex: The Founding of Three Schools

Within 25 years of his arrival in Sussex, Woodard had founded and established three new schools in virgin and stunning sites – Lancing dramatically poised high on the South Downs, looking across the Adur valley to Shoreham and its port and beyond to the sea; Hurstpierpoint tucked into the Sussex plain with its splendid backcloth of the scarp slope of the Downs; and Ardingly, on a hillside in the woods of the Weald, looking down to the meadows of the Ouse valley and beyond to the London to Brighton railway viaduct. Views and settings matter to schools and in this regard Woodard had a finely tuned eye.

The very low fees helped. Fifteen guineas per year at Ardingly, and 18 guineas at Hurstpierpoint were affordable to many of those parents who had not previously considered a boarding education for their children. London and its satellite towns were growing fast, and railways enabled its clerks, tradesmen and professional classes to send them to these schools. The London Brighton and South Coast Railway Company, with its distinctive chocolate brown and yellow livery, played a big part in the life of Woodard's schoolboys.

However, shoe-string economics can have unintended consequences. All three schools were opened before their buildings were complete and proper services installed. There was much skimping on the building of Hurstpierpoint and it was not as solid as it looked when it opened its doors in June 1853. The College of SS Mary and Nicolas moved to Lancing Hill in August 1857 and there were no classrooms, no studies, no chapel and no gymnasium. The sanitation for 180 boys was inadequate. Life was bleak. Mistakes were made and three boys drowned whilst bathing in the river Adur in 1858. Ardingly was a shell with no running water when it opened its doors on 28 July 1870, and within six weeks five boys had died of scarlet fever.

11   *Hurstpierpoint College: aerial view. The first of Woodard's new school buildings, opened in 1853, nestling in the vale of Sussex beneath the scarp slope of the South Downs.*

12   *Ardingly College: aerial view. Gloriously located high amidst the steeply wooded hills and farms of the Sussex Weald, Ardingly was the jewel in Woodard's crown, creating a haven of opportunity for the sons of the tradesmen classes.*

13 *Lancing College: aerial view. Monastic in its apparent remoteness on the Downs, Woodard had a finely tuned eye for the setting of a school. Pevsner approves: 'High up on a beautiful exposed site above the Adur. Some atonement for the many heaps of ugliness which the 19th century uploaded blindly on the English landscape'.*

Strong leadership was essential in these pioneering communities. At Hurstpierpoint, Edward Lowe was Woodard's most trusted lieutenant. Son of a Liverpool solicitor, he, like Woodard, had had no formal schooling, and like him had found a place at Magdalen Hall and been profoundly influenced by the Oxford Movement. He was a vigorous and energetic headmaster for the first 23 years of Hurstpierpoint's existence, laying sure foundations and establishing traditions which survive to this day. As the first of Woodard's new school buildings, it was the launching pad and it was Lowe who made it work. It was a huge achievement to pay off its debts by 1861 and by 1869 it housed 364 pupils. He was a great supporter of the boys and forged strong links with the local community and the Old Boys. More of an educationalist than Woodard, he was the only person capable of standing up to him. Later he was to be Provost of Denstone for 19 years and finally succeeded Woodard as Provost of Lancing and of the Society when the Founder died in 1891.

The Reverend Frederick Mertens was equally important at Ardingly, devoting his whole professional life to founding the community in Shoreham, masterminding the move and then completing the new building. Devout, hard-working, resilient in the face of many tribulations, his 36 years as Ardingly's first headmaster ensured that this jewel in the Woodard crown surmounted all manner of financial obstacles to become firmly established.

14   *Henry Martin Gibbs (1850-1928). Philanthropist, whose Lancing education shaped his life, his contribution was absolutely essential to the Woodard cause. This photo was taken in his last year at the school.*

The lack of such leadership at Lancing meant that its start was much less convincing. Three heads in the space of three years who, for whatever reason, were not up to the job, meant that it was not until the arrival of the experienced, forceful and absolutely committed the Reverend Robert Sanderson in 1861 that the School began to grow. But it was not only the lack of effective leadership that contributed to Lancing's uncertain start. It was in effect an upper class school and that was an anomaly in the Society that was dedicated to providing a cheap education for the middle classes.

There were constant financial pressures. Woodard though was a determined and effective fundraiser. He had a core of highly committed supporters who believed in the work he was doing. Chief amongst these was Henry Martin Gibbs (1850-1928), scion of the family which had made its fortune in the Peruvian guano trade in the first part of the 19th century. They were the leading benefactors of the Oxford Movement, funding 19 churches, and Keble College, in addition to these schools. The grand family house at Tyntesfield, near Bristol, is another monument to this great wealth. Gibbs, an old boy of Lancing, was 28 when his father died and he took an enormous interest in Woodard's work. Without his financial support it is unlikely that Ardingly would have got off the ground.

Woodard was a man for big occasions; the laying of a foundation stone, the opening of a school, and the dedication of a new chapel were all opportunities to be exploited. The formula was simple and effective. Carefully focused invitations were sent to the great, the good and those who were believed to have well-stocked bank accounts. Following an elaborate High Church ceremony with benches of robed bishops and other senior churchmen, the party would sit down to a grand luncheon. There would be speeches, not least in explaining what still needed to be financed. At the end of proceedings there would be one point of exit. All would be given a card and envelope. Those who were not able to make a pledge that day would be followed up methodically, indeed remorselessly. On one famous, perhaps notorious, occasion, no one was allowed to leave the room until the £15,000 outstanding on that particular project had been pledged.

But even Woodard could not stage-manage everything. The *Brighton Herald*, for example, was very critical of the amount of alcohol consumed at the ceremony following the formal launch of building operations at Lancing in 1855. Woodard's ventures aroused strong support from his devoted followers and vociferous opposition from those who were fearful of their High Church character.

There were several major stand-alone fund-raising meetings, and not all of them achieved their desired end. The 26-year-old Robert Cecil, later to become Prime Minister as Lord Salisbury, chaired the meeting held in Brighton Town Hall to raise funds for the new school buildings on Lancing Hill on 2 December 1856. He made some pertinent points in his opening address: '... he went on to warn his hearers that our commercial supremacy will not descend from generation to generation like an heirloom without exertion, but needs the constant support of minds disciplined by the study of mechanics and chemistry. America is already abreast with us in the commercial contest, and America vigorously educates all its citizens.' But then the question of confession was raised from the floor and when it was referred to Woodard he refused to answer it. He was not good in these situations and not for the last time there was harm done to the cause as the meeting ended in rowdy tumult, as fears of Popery and Rome came to the fore. No matter the fact, there was a belief that systematic confession was practised in his schools. Subsequently the *Brighton Herald* published a letter entitled '*Puseyism at Shoreham*' – '... to swear fidelity and receive wages from our church, while enforcing the doctrine of its antagonist is the basest and most dangerous dishonesty.'

Several big meetings were planned for 1861. At St James' Hall in London, for example, there was an impressive array of dignitaries on the platform – Lord Brougham in the chair, Longley, Archbishop of York, John Walter, Editor of *The Times*, Lord Redesdale, William Cotton, formerly Governor of the Bank of England, and Ashurst Turner Gilbert, Bishop of Chichester. Lord Salisbury chaired the subsequent London Committee which raised £25,000 and there were also local committees in Brighton, south London, Lewes, Cuckfield and Bognor.

The meeting at the Sheldonian Theatre in Oxford later in the year was less successful. The vice- chancellor of the University was in the chair. Gladstone spoke at length: 'I do not believe that this age has given a more remarkable example of great energy, great constructive power, and a perfect mastery of what I may call the machinery of philanthropic agitation, of the most entire judgement and admirable tact in confronting difficulties, and of the great gift of winning confidence, than we have seen in the operations of Mr Woodard since first he laid his hand to the task.' He was followed by Lord Salisbury. The meeting was packed but on the way in Dr Golightly, Fellow of Jesus College, had been handing out leaflets claiming that confession was practised in the Woodard schools. Again, Woodard failed to take the opportunity to respond to these accusations and allay fears and this did great harm to the Society. The vice-chancellor withdrew his support and Oxford was no longer fruitful territory.

Wherever he went Woodard aroused strong feelings, as Basil Handford, the historian of Lancing, commented: 'Opposed and misunderstood and often disliked, he won from his friends a passionate loyalty and even from his critics a grudging admiration.'

The meeting at the Town Hall in Cambridge in 1864 was held in support of the school being planned at Ardingly for 1,000 pupils. It just about paid its way and enabled the foundation stone to be laid later that year by Earl Granville, President of the Privy Council. Again this was a splendid Woodard occasion. Moving amongst the guests the Provost is alleged to have said: 'This is like Heaven. Many whom I confidently expected to meet are absent, and many surprise me by their presence.' His sense of humour was undimmed.

Woodard was no politician and he was either unwilling or unable to counter the criticisms made of the religious tone of his schools. His doctrinal and partisan approach to the Christian life meant that there was little room for disagreement. The complaint by a member of staff at Hurstpierpoint, John Hewett, that there was systematic and compulsory confession at the school both in its original home in New Shoreham and in its temporary premises in the village of Hurstpierpoint led to a Visitation by the bishop in 1853. The bishop found that boys were allowed to confess if they felt the need at some particular time, that they were discouraged from confessing regularly, and were not allowed to confess at all without their parents' leave. Although this could not have exonerated the school more fully, there was still a widespread belief in some circles that confession was compulsory in Woodard's schools. Interestingly, 12 years later, Hewett in a fit of remorse, wrote to the Provost beseeching his pardon for the trouble he had caused.

Another dispute was with a near neighbour, the Reverend John Goring of Wiston. In 1850 Goring had offered financial support to the Society but in return wanted some say in how the money was to be spent. Woodard, resolute and autocratic to the core, refused to countenance this and there followed a lengthy correspondence which also included the bishop. Six years later, following the controversy surrounding the Brighton fundraising meeting, Goring went to the press who published the earlier correspondence. There was further unseemly publicity.

Although Woodard accomplished great things in the school world, he spent only three years as a curate in Shoreham. In 1850 he resigned his post in order to devote all of his time and considerable energies to his work as Provost of the Society of St Nicolas. His family moved into rented accommodation and then to 12 Cannon Place, Brighton where they remained for 12 years. It was convenient for the railway station but it was no coincidence that Cannon Place, then a fashionable address in Brighton, was just around the corner from St Paul's Church, Arthur Wagner's High Church creation, which had been designed by the older Richard Carpenter responsible also for both Hurstpierpoint and Lancing. Throughout his life Woodard was never happier than in the company of fellow Anglo-Catholics who also provided the basis of many of his professional relationships.

Then in 1862 the family moved to the substantial Martyn Lodge in Henfield, a village just north of the Downs, eight miles from Brighton and easily accessible to Lancing and Hurstpierpoint. This was to be his home for the rest of his life.

He worked hard. As we have seen he was also autocratic and kept personal control of all aspects of the business of the Society of St Nicolas. There was no proper constitution, no accounts were published and few records kept. There are occasional references to his position in the records of the individual schools. In

1870, for example, Hurstpierpoint contributed £290 to his annual salary, and there were suggestions that he was earning at least £900 p.a (approximately £60,000 today). Suffice it to say that Woodard was able to purchase Martyn Lodge and significantly his four sons were all educated at Lancing.

Like so many great achievers he was a driven man. He was also much in demand. As early as 1850 Bishop Blomfield tried to persuade him to become involved in the middle-grade schools in London, and was even prepared to transfer to him the Diocesan Association of London with its attendant funds. It was a measure of the respect in which he was held. Two other dioceses approached him in connection with their plans for launching middle-grade schools. He was consulted, too, by both the Italian and Russian governments as they sought to develop comprehensive schemes of education. And later in the 1870s the Bishop of Dunedin in New Zealand was keen that he should go out there to advise on his scheme. It was a step too far, even for Woodard.

The year 1868 was important in the Woodard scheme of things. The laying of the foundation stone of Lancing Chapel saw the Woodard ceremonial machine in full flow – 300 clergy, a choir of 300, representatives from all the schools, and an address by the Bishop of Oxford. No wonder that the *Manchester Guardian* wrote 'many hearts beat very hard …'. Yet at the same time there were some who were concerned by the scale of the undertaking and its cost, not least as the architect's plans showed a 350-foot tower at its western end. Ardingly was not yet half built, and there was still a need for essential educational and domestic facilities at Lancing and Hurstpierpoint, all of which required financing. No one was quite sure where the money was going to come from for any of these projects.

SEVEN

Canon of Manchester

The year 1870 was to be a turning point in Woodard's own life and in the direction of his grand design. His passion and sense of mission showed no sign of dimming and the opening of Ardingly, in its new though unfinished buildings, meant that the initial three grade structure was established in Sussex. Now his eyes and those of his supporters were being drawn to the Midlands and North of the country, the heartland of industrial Britain. It was with this aim in mind that Prime Minister Gladstone used his powers of patronage to place Woodard in a well rewarded canonry at Manchester Cathedral. It gave Woodard the opportunity and scope to develop his schools in new areas. And in the same year his old university, Oxford, awarded him the honorary degree of DCL (Doctor of Civil Law). For a man who had only achieved a pass degree, this was a notable mark of recognition. He was becoming a national figure.

There were, however, obstacles and in the event the 1870s and '80s were to prove less fruitful as an environment for his founding of new private schools than the pioneering years of the 1850s and '60s. There were several reasons for this.

First and foremost was competition from the reformed endowed schools. When Woodard started his great work the majority of the Tudor and Stuart endowed foundations were moribund. Their curriculum was limited to the classics, too often the trustees neglected their duties, and in many cases the endowments had been appropriated by idle and negligent priests. There were few pupils.

Reform, however, was in the air and, indeed, implemented in the army, the civil service, and at Oxford and Cambridge Universities. In 1861 the Clarendon Commission reported on what were known as the Great Nine public schools: Eton, Harrow, Winchester, Westminster, Shrewsbury, Merchant Taylors', Rugby, Charterhouse and St Paul's. The Endowed Schools Enquiry chaired by Lord

Taunton was established in 1865, and reported in 1868, paving the way for the Endowed Schools Act of 1869. This was to prove the most profound interference by government in the charitable world since the dissolution of the monasteries by Henry VIII. The ancient trusts had to show evidence that they were fulfilling their aims, and the Commissioners had the power to combine trusts, and to reallocate endowments. The result was that many schools which had lain dormant were revived and new ones created. From now on inexpensive day schools in the towns and suburbs came to provide serious competition to the independent boarding schools. Steyning Grammar School with boarding provision was just a few miles from Lancing and Hurstpierpoint; and in 1887-8 the Worshipful Company of Skinners founded the Skinners' Middle School in Tunbridge Wells with fees of £15 p.a. and a number of bursaries, and also Sir Andrew Judd's Commercial School in Tonbridge with a day fee of £8 p.a. In addition, for many parents there was the added attraction that these new and re-created foundations were free from any religious restrictions.

This was accompanied by the founding of the Church Schools Company in 1883 which established day schools, including a conscience clause so that parents could opt out of religious worship. Archbishop Benson and many other bishops supported this. Predictably Woodard could not agree: 'I know of nothing so damaging to the character of English churchmanship as the archbishop's move.' Yet in this instance there was an enduring truth in what Woodard had to say: 'For a religious environment is never without its influence. A boy may leave school apparently unaffected, or even alienated, by the services he has attended and the instruction he has received. Yet, little though he may recognise the fact, he will have been in contact with something assured, unchanging, and victoriously dynamic; and the memory of it, at later moments of his life, when passion is violent, temptation overwhelming, or despair insistent, may avail to call him home to a Church which offers the power and grace promised by God Himself in Christ.' The routines of the Church year, discipline and structures, wonderful stories of the Bible, calming and uplifting beauty of the music, and atmosphere of the great chapels, especially when lit by candlelight, seeped into the souls of countless Woodard pupils.

A second great challenge was the financial bottomless pit of Lancing College Chapel whose foundation stone had been laid in 1868. Religion was, of course, central to the life of Woodard's schools and Lancing was his flagship. At the very heart of his scheme he wanted a magnificent monument which would send out a message to all. It was hugely expensive, and all the parents in his schools were levied towards its cost. 'It was out of proportion to its purpose; an act of reckless extravagance hampering the future work of the Society; an act of faith; an expression of a consecrated aestheticism,' said one critic. Woodard tried to justify himself at the dedication of the Crypt for use as a chapel in 1875: 'The great chapel as it will be hereafter, is, I know, open to the criticisms of those who only look at

15 *Carol service in Hurstpierpoint Chapel. Fine music in splendid chapels is a hallmark of Woodard's schools especially on cold winter's nights in candle lit services; a theatre for the great music of the Christian church to raise the spirits and calm the troubled soul.*

it as a chapel for a school of 300 or 400 boys; but, to those who regard it in its true character as the central chapel of a great Society, consecrated to a noble effort for the defence and support of Christian truth, as represented to us by the Church of our country, it will not appear to violate the rules of modesty and prudence, but rather the faith in the essential strength of the Church of those who promote it.'

Woodard himself appreciated what a millstone it had become when he wrote in 1880: 'My great desire now is to be free to spend the remainder of my time and money in building lower middle schools. But this I cannot do until I can free myself of Lancing College Chapel. It is a necessity that we should have this large and costly building at the centre of so great a national work, but it has for the time hindered other important work.' It was not dedicated until 1911 by which time it is estimated to have cost £300,000, a staggering sum by any measure. The west end was still not completed. In 1947 the Friends of Lancing Chapel commissioned a new design for it from Stephen Dykes Bower. The west wall and rose window were eventually dedicated in 1978, but to this day the building still remains unfinished. The Friends of Lancing Chapel have recently drawn up new plans for its completion by the building of a porch at the west end.

A third hindrance was Woodard's autocratic style. He dominated the Chapter which was the governing body of the Society. There was no proper constitution, no records were kept, and no accounts maintained. Although the Society of St Nicolas had been founded in 1848, and although nearly £250,000 had been raised in the next 20 years, there was no Finance Committee until 1863, and no Bursar till 1871. Woodard's son, Billy, was appointed as Custos and Steward of Lands and Properties in 1868. Woodard stubbornly resisted any attempts to interfere in *his* organisation of *his* schools.

All this meant that there was a lack of suitably qualified and independent-minded people sitting on the Chapter. Too many were overly compliant, invited to serve because they came from the right religious stock and also, it must be

said, because they would be no threat to the Provost. Strategic planning was neglected and Woodard acting alone made some poor decisions, not least some of his appointments – three heads in the first three years at Lancing meant that the College had a most uncertain start. Awdry in succession to Lowe at Hurstpierpoint was simply not up to the job and in his six years there pupil numbers fell from 306 to 166. He was, however, unlucky to face competition from Ardingly following its opening in 1870 at half Hurstpierpoint's fees, and the agricultural depression of the 1870s which hit hard the Sussex farmers. Later McKenzie at Lancing, in succession to Sanderson, was unable to work with the system of dyarchy whereby the chaplain was appointed separately by the provost and was responsible to him. Sometimes this worked but all too often there was systemic tension between the head and the chaplain.

The buccaneering and instinctive approach in the pioneering days may have been appropriate. The lack of a proper corporate structure meant, however, that the Woodard family of schools was ill-equipped to cope as the schools moved into the mature stage of the cycle of business development. It is one thing to found an institution, but a very different challenge to create the necessary consolidation in order to ensure self-sustaining growth.

Woodard's connections with Manchester were slim. He accepted a substantial stipend of £2,000 p.a. but the records show that throughout his 21 years as a canon he only attended one meeting in four of the Cathedral Chapter. In 1882 he was appointed Sub Dean of the Cathedral and in 1888 Rector of St Philip's, Salford. Two curates were employed here and Woodard preached only once! There were elements of Trollopian practices in the cathedral close and it was ironic that Woodard himself could be accused of the laxness and absenteeism which had encouraged the reforming Oxford Movement all those years before which had provided him with so much inspiration.

Given the limited responsibilities of a canon in a cathedral chapter, Woodard continued to live 250 miles away at the family home in Henfield. Martyn Lodge was a sizeable family residence set in several acres of grounds on the edge of the village and within a stone's throw of the parish church. Six resident staff were recorded in the 1871 Census – a housekeeper, cook, housemaid, kitchen maid, groom and carpenter – and, with several of his children living at home, this made for a large (and expensive) household.

It was also a lively and sociable home. 'He was exceedingly hospitable to all sorts and conditions of man. Every Christmas all the communicants in the parish were

16   *Martyn Lodge, Henfield in 2011. Woodard's home from 1862 till his death 29 years later. A few miles from Lancing and Hurstpierpoint, it was the residence of a Victorian churchman of significance.*

entertained at a feast. He had a talent for banter which his guests appreciated, and nonetheless for the punch which he delighted to mix and ladle out to them on these occasions,' wrote his son-in-law, Sir John Otter.

But if Gladstone had hoped Woodard would be able to use Manchester Cathedral as a supportive base for these schools he had not reckoned with his rigidity and dogmatism. It was not long before he fell out with the Bishop of Manchester, Fraser. They clashed in particular over his fundraising activities and also a sermon, allegedly espousing confession, which Woodard gave in 1875: 'I feel that I am not called upon to waste my time in a needless controversy at the instigation of a gentleman (the person who had complained) who has no right to demand it, and also is evidently ignorant of the subject on which he writes,' wrote Woodard in response to the Bishop's request for a copy of the text of the sermon. Fortunately the Bishop was restrained in his response: 'I can only hope on a subject so mysterious, and on which considerable latitude has been allowed in the Church of England, his language may have been misunderstood.'

Fraser was one of the great Victorian bishops. He was very active in creating new parishes and setting up schools to serve the densely packed working classes in the diocese which had only been created in 1847. He came, too, from the old High Church tradition and so was suspicious of the Oxford Movement and its ritualism. Like Bishop Blomfield in East London before him, Fraser was annoyed by Woodard's obscurantism and was determined not to be distracted by him from his more important works. Woodard's relationship with Fraser was neither happy nor fruitful.

Woodard was at his best in conceiving and executing big schemes. For several years he worked on plans for a new cathedral in Manchester on a site he had earmarked in Piccadilly in the heart of the city. The young Herbert Carpenter was the architect and the plans showed an octagonal tower as at Ely. It would have been one of the largest Gothic churches in Europe. In the event the equally large funds required to build it were beyond even Woodard and perhaps wisely the plans were quietly dropped in 1878. Northern hard-headed business thinking regarded a huge cathedral as draining funds from the other and important Anglican works which were being created in the diocese. Woodard had been checked in a way that had not happened with Lancing Chapel.

He was on surer grounds with his schools. The creation of Denstone College was under way when he was appointed to the Manchester Canonry. Sir Percival Heywood and Henry Meynell, Vicar of Denstone, were the two key figures here in the founding of this Middle Middle school close to Uttoxeter in Staffordshire, equivalent to Hurstpierpoint. Heywood offered a site and a large donation in memory of his son who had recently died, whilst Meynell was the forceful and energetic parish priest. It was to be the centre of a new division, the Society of SS Mary and John, Lichfield.

A formal appeal was launched in Manchester for funding 'A Midland Counties and Manchester Public School for sons of persons of small means.' Predictably, however, Bishop Fraser would not support 'such a divisive measure likely to lead to partisanship.' In addition it should be noted that Trent College had been opened in 1868 at Long Eaton in Nottinghamshire to counteract the High Church schools. Woodard was undaunted; indeed, he relished the challenge. In 1872 at a meeting at Queen's Hall, Manchester, he was able to raise £20,000 at one of his trademark grand luncheons. And later in the year a luncheon at Uttoxeter for 600, followed by a party at Alton Towers (then an ancestral home rather than the modern day theme park), hosted by the Earl of Shrewsbury and supported in particular by O.E. Coope, brewer in Burton, raised £5,000. The Bishop of Lichfield preached at the Dedication of the College in 1873: 'The great question is now before us. It is brought home to our hearts. The battle is begun. We have conscience clauses excluding all distinctive teaching. We have a powerful league clamouring for our banishment ...' The College opened in 1877 with fees of £34 p.a. The chapel was dedicated in 1887, and the dining hall completed in 1891, by which time £100,000 had been spent on the buildings and the community firmly established.

17   *Denstone College Chapel. Incorporated into the characteristic H-shape, the chapel by Herbert Carpenter and his partner Benjamin Ingelow was begun in 1879, two years after the College opened, and consecrated in 1887.*

Meanwhile Lord Brownlow had offered 60 acres and a donation of £1,000 to set Ellesmere College in north Shropshire on its way as a Lower Middle school, equivalent to Ardingly. Brownlow was a landowner and politician. MP for North Shropshire until he succeeded to the title which included the great wealth of the Bridgewater estate, he served as a member of the House of Lords in Lord Salisbury's government in the 1880s. Woodard immediately set about forming a fundraising committee in Manchester. The foundation stone was laid in 1879 and the College opened in 1884 with fees of £15 p.a. Predictably it was opposed by the evangelicals, as *The Rock*, their leading journal, expounded: '… we think that we have said quite enough to satisfy our Shropshire friends that the less they have to do with Canon Woodard's schools the better. In fact, unless the movement be arrested it will end in placing the whole education of the middle classes in the hands of the Lancing Jesuits.' Ellesmere's start was slower but it was not long before it, too, was soundly established although it was not until 1928 that its chapel was completed.

In 1878 Woodard's attention was drawn to difficulties at Taunton College, a private school built on a spacious site on the edge of this prosperous market town in Somerset. It was inadequately funded and in 1879 he was offered the total property for £12,500. He bided his time and the mortgagees repossessed the 14-acre campus and put it up for auction. Woodard turned up incognito, saw that there were no other bidders and was able to purchase it privately a few weeks later for £8,000.

18   *Denstone College. 'The site is fine, the composition is sweeping and has never been destroyed. Gothic of the Middle Pointed kind, and not at all ornamental,' says Pevsner.*

19 & 20   *Ellesmere College. A school in all seasons.*
Built 1879-84 by Carpenter and Ingelow, by now the
Woodard house style was well established.

21   *The main school buildings of King's College, Taunton. Here in 1879 Woodard purchased an existing school, Taunton College, which had gone bankrupt. The main school buildings (in the Gothic style by C.E. Giles, 1867-9) fitted very naturally into the Woodard landscape.*

His eye for a good deal was as sharp as ever. Immediately he installed the second master of Hurstpierpoint as the head and the School was re-opened in 1880 as a full member of the Society, and re-named King's College, Taunton.

King's did not have an easy start and numbers were invariably a problem, not least because Taunton was over-supplied with private secondary schools. Its membership of the Woodard family of schools and in particular the financial support of Henry Martin Gibbs helped it to ride these economic storms and in due course become a successful and self-sufficient entity.

Another change which was to perplex Woodard was the slow and belated emergence of girls' education. Fundamentally he believed that his life's work was the education of boys. Following the opening of Cheltenham Ladies College in 1853 however, Woodard was persuaded to become involved with Miss Rooper's private boarding school in Hove. Aided by its first Warden, Lady Caroline Eliot, he settled the school at Bognor in 1855 under the name of St Michael's. Tellingly it was regarded as an associate, rather than a full member of the Society.

In 1872, importantly, the Girls' Public Day School Company (GPDSC) was founded to establish schools which would provide a sound academic education at a price which most middle class families could afford. They were in fact aimed at just the sort of people whom Woodard was trying to reach although they were day, rather than boarding, schools and they were non-denominational.

In most respects girls' education was a step too far for Woodard and an opportunity was missed. He was conservative to the core, as witnessed in this letter in 1880: 'Public schools for girls are of very doubtful merit. Religious houses or convents are more in harmony with my ideas … The High School system, and knowledge without the grace of female gentleness and devotion, is another cloud in the gathering storm which is awaiting society. So far as we have gone with girls' schools it is all very well, but the question is shall we commit ourselves to a general scheme? The banners of St Michael and St Anne might be at our gathering at Taunton, to show that we will do what we can, but so slippery are women that we must watch our own progress before we promise more.' This does not read well today but we should not forget that he was a child of his age.

In fact Lowe did play a significant part in extending schools for girls when he was Provost of the Midland Division of the Society. St Anne's, Abbots Bromley, where his sister was Headmistress, was founded in 1874, and incorporated with SS Mary and John in 1890. Today it is the Abbots Bromley School for Girls; and also incidentally the home of the offices of the Woodard Corporation.

Some time after Woodard's death, the Northern Division was created in 1903 with schools such as Queen Margaret's, Scarborough (hit by shelling from German battleships in 1914), Queen Ethelburga's at Harrogate, and a prep school at Duncombe Park, Helmsley. Then in the Western Division, St Katherine's at Hatherton Park, near Taunton, was founded in 1922, and St Claire's at Polwithen, outside Penzance at the same time.

In fact girls' independent boarding education was always going to be difficult in the 20th century especially in small rural communities. Apart from the large and renowned boarding schools such as Roedean, Wycombe Abbey, Cheltenham Ladies College, and Benenden, the market for girls' independent education was clearly in the urban and suburban day schools where the GPDSC had established its roots. Woodard's strong belief in the all-embracing benefits of boarding meant that he had less faith in day schools. He had missed the opportunity.

EIGHT

Last Days in Henfield

The great Victorians did not always find it easy to wind down as the middle and later years of life crept up on them. The energy and intensity which are required for the founding of grand enterprises do not necessarily enable the consolidation which ensures development into maturity. Brunel overstretched himself with his *Great Eastern* steam ship, Livingstone found life as an explorer amongst the native Africans more rewarding than the missionary he set out to be, and Florence Nightingale became a bedridden *grande dame* for the last 20 years of her life.

Nathaniel Woodard, too, found consolidation more difficult in an environment which became increasingly competitive. The Endowed Schools Act of 1869 unlocked the resources of many ancient trusts for the purpose of providing good secondary education at a cost affordable to many. The consequent competition to Woodard's schools was significant. The rise of nonconformity and a more open religious society was an affront to his deep seated Anglo-Catholic beliefs. His autocratic style was not only out of tune in an increasingly democratic age but also meant that the Chapter of the Society, its over-arching governing body, lacked the freedom, initiative and confidence to respond to the challenges of the school market place. His longstanding associates were defensive and conservative in their disposition, seeing this changing environment as a threat rather than an opportunity; and Lancing Chapel was an ever present millstone around his neck.

Nonetheless Woodard tried to press on. St Oswald's College, Ellesmere had been opened in 1884 with 70 boys. Slowly but surely it established foundations and began to grow though it was not until the 1920s that it became formally known as Ellesmere College. In the same year, Lowe was given permission to found St Augustine's in Dewsbury, West Yorkshire, but, after five heads in 15 years, the School was closed in 1899. Significantly the neighbouring Wheelwright's Grammar School was well endowed and a much better prospect. The lesson to be learned from this episode was that local authorities in association with the reformed endowed foundations could establish secondary schools throughout the land.

Also in 1884 Woodard wrote to all Lancing pupils past and present, requesting their financial support of his Lower Middle schools. The tone of his letter was forthright. He believed that the old public schools of England, often founded by kings and bishops, had originally been intended for teaching the sound faith to those who could benefit. Now they had become rich and secularised. He urged Lancing's alumni to help and attach themselves in heart and soul to the work of SS Mary & Nicolas College in providing for those less well off, the lower middle classes: 'I wish you to consider them, not only as deserving of this help, but as a class among whom lies buried some of its brightest intellects and loftiest souls ... Take care of the training of the Middle Classes and you take care, at the same time, of the best interests of the Nation.'

It was perhaps not wholly surprising that there was very little response to this letter and 15 years later in 1899 the Association of Lancing Old Boys was wound up and its few funds given to Ardingly College.

22   *Worksop College. On the edge of the Duke of Newcastle's 30,000 acre Clumber Estate, Worksop was the last of the Carpenter designed schools with their characteristic H block and Gothic towers.*

In 1890 the Society accepted from the Duke of Newcastle 150 acres of the Clumber Estate in Sherwood Forest in Nottinghamshire as a home for what was to become the sixth Woodard school, St Cuthbert's College, Worksop. Richard Portland, the 7th Duke, was a devout Anglo-Catholic, had recently been married at its London heart, All Saints, Margaret Street, and immediately employed G.F. Bodley to design a magnificent Gothic church close to his ancestral home, Clumber House. Then he turned his attention to the proposed school. Sadly Woodard was too ill to attend the laying of the foundation stone that year. It was in fact the Reverend Henry Meynell, Vicar of Denstone, Prebendary of Lichfield and Provost of the Midland Division from 1891, who took over the torch from Woodard and made St Cuthbert's happen. He was its driving force, arranging fund-raising meetings at which he preached throughout the East Midlands and the North, handling the details of negotiations with the Duke of Newcastle, liaising with the architect, Herbert Carpenter, and builders. Woodard had written to him in 1887: 'To whom do we owe so much as you!! A stranger sent to me by God.' And when Meynell died in 1903 the *Cuthbertian* wrote: 'If the Midland Branch of the Woodard Schools owes much to him, it may be truly said that we owe our existence to him, for it was mainly through his zeal and energy, that St Cuthbert's was founded.'

23   *Abbots Bromley Chapel. Another Capenter and Ingelow creation, built between 1875 and 1881.*

24   *Abbots Bromley Chapel interior. Radio 4 live Daily Service sung by the choir.*

The School opened in 1895 though it was not till 1911 that its superb chapel designed by Sir Aston Webb and financed by Viscount Mountgarret was dedicated.

Woodard had in fact in 1886 made his last public visit to Hurstpierpoint, a mere five miles from his Henfield home and close to his heart as the first of his new school buildings. Increasingly, old age and infirmity confined him to his home and the last five years of his life were not always easy.

Eliza, his wife and the mother of his five surviving children, had died in 1873. About her we know little. The 15,000 letters in the Woodard archive at Lancing are mostly to do with the business matters of the Society of St Nicolas. Perhaps it tells us something about Woodard's personality that there are not many references to personal or private matters. There is no evidence that she ever appeared at grand occasions at the schools on high or holy days although the *Hurst Johnian* does mention her attendance at school plays and Volunteers' Balls. We can merely conjecture that she was an ever-present wife and mother in the family home perhaps complementing her husband's driven personality. She must, too, have been patient and tolerant, not least in having her dining room in New Shoreham Vicarage taken over as a classroom. Having played an important part in the whole Woodard enterprise it is reassuring to know that she is still

Nathaniel Woodard DCL Priest Founder of S Nicolas College born March

25   *Woodard's Vault at Lancing. Designed by Temple Moore, the recumbent bronze effigy is by P. Bryant Baker (1916). Erroneously Woodard's date of birth is inscribed as 1810.*

remembered today at Worksop where the Headmaster's house is named in her memory as Elizabeth House.

In 1888 Woodard was struck a devastating blow when his eldest son, Mortimer, died. Soldier, parliamentary candidate, and later barrister on the North Eastern Circuit, he was close to his father and it had long been intended that he should take up the reins at the heart of the Society's affairs at such time when his father died.

George, his second son, was also a soldier, serving as a Colonel in the 2nd Queen's Royal Foot Regiment but does not appear to have played a part in his father's enterprises.

His third son, William, known always as Billy, had been a pupil at Lancing for 11 years (1850-61), was an undergraduate at Cambridge and then returned to Sussex to spend the rest of his life working for his father. Custos and Steward of Lands and Property from 1868 until his death in 1918, he was in effect bursar of the Society, responsible for all the new buildings and repairs in the Southern Division which included the building of Ardingly and much of the Lancing Chapel. He was a self-taught clerk of works and his achievements as a builder were astonishing. His role in the Woodard venture was absolutely essential.

Lambert was a priest at the High Anglican church of St Paul's, Bedford, and incidentally the grandfather of Sir Robert Woodard after whom the newly opened Academy in Lancing village is named.

Finally the youngest child, and only daughter, Audrey, was to marry Sir John Otter in 1889 and it was he who wrote a biography of the Founder in 1925.

Curiously in 1890, aged 79, Woodard married his housekeeper, Dorothy Poritt, aged 23, the daughter of a schoolmaster. The marriage took place at All Saints, Margaret Street, Marylebone. Tantalisingly we know nothing about the background and circumstances of this marriage. His daughter, Audrey, had left home to marry and Woodard was infirm and could not survive on his own, especially in such a large house. Perhaps Victorian propriety meant that the only way a single woman could live in the same home was to marry him. Whatever the truth, the situation seemed bizarre. In any event within ten months Woodard had died. It is in some respects reassuring to know that two years later his widow was re-married to a man of her own generation, an accountant.

She was not, however, poor. Two months before he died, Woodard had signed a new will (dated 11 February 1891) leaving Martyn Lodge, his horse and carriage, books, wine and plate to Dorothy. What his children thought about Dorothy's substantial inheritance is not recorded. His will also left 13 cottages in Henfield to his daughter, Audrey, and all remaining monies to his sons. Again there is no record of contemporary clerical opinion about the wealth accumulated during his life as a priest.

Woodard died on 21 April 1891. He was buried in the vault of the Chapel at Lancing and by all accounts it was a moving and sombre occasion. All the key figures in the Woodard world, together with representatives from all his schools, were there, many having travelled long distances. A Supplement to the *Lancing College Magazine*, June 1891 reads as follows: 'The history of St Nicolas College shews what may be done for the accomplishment of a great end by the efforts of one man if his whole soul is thrown into his work, if he has the courage of his convictions, will spare neither himself or his means, and will not allow himself to be daunted by opposition. Such a man was Nathaniel Woodard.'

NINE
His Legacy

Nathaniel Woodard died a disappointed man. He had not accomplished his avowed aim of creating a national system of Church schools for the middle classes within the means of most of them. What he had done was nonetheless remarkable; it was to create 10 schools and collectively join them together as a teaching order in the Anglo-Catholic tradition of the Church of England, the Society of St Nicolas.

Although well known and respected in his own field, Woodard could not be considered a household name, and in any event it had become widely accepted that only the State had the resources and authority to establish a national and comprehensive system of secondary education. Forster's Education Act (1870) was a milestone in the expansion of State education, a clear marker of things to come. The Woodard schools had been launched certainly but without endowments they were adrift and left to fend for themselves in an environment which had become increasingly infertile.

Woodard's most creative period had been in the 1850s and '60s. It was then that his schools were most needed. They paved the way and showed what was possible. These were pioneering days and funds were available. Subsequently the reform of the endowed schools created competition and funds began to dry up. There were further challenges ahead, as the State began to provide secondary education following the Acts of 1899 and 1902, especially the latter which made schooling from 11 to 14 compulsory. Its own grammar schools, and in particular the direct grant schools from 1907, were in direct competition with the cheaper end of the public school market. In addition, agricultural depression in the 1870s and '80s, together with increasing competition from the newly industrialising Germany, France and the USA, provided significant economic challenges, and consequent loss of income for the middle classes for whom the Woodard schools were intended. All of this helps to explain why there was a serious fall in pupil numbers; for example, from 200 to 90 at Lancing (1886-99), and at Hurstpierpoint from 211 to 128 (1896-1903).

No individual, of course, could have any control over such fundamental and overwhelming external factors. Woodard did not, however, leave an easy or straightforward inheritance. He had been a domineering and autocratic provost and the Chapter had at times shown mistaken loyalty to him. When he died the Society was still governed by draft statutes dating back to 1848. It lacked the structure and authority, together with leadership with the necessary expertise and capacity to move speedily to address the challenges, and indeed exploit the opportunities, which were to arise. His designated successor as provost, Lowe, was equally conservative and driven by the priority of maintaining the theological purity of the Society. He was strongly supported by Blackmore, the financial secretary, and Billy Woodard. It was not until the passing of these three 'old guard' pillars of the Society (Blackmore died in 1909, Lowe in 1912 and Billy Woodard in 1918), that the traditional Woodard philosophy and way of doing things came to an end. Now the path was clear for a new and fresh approach.

Lowe did, however, have the good sense to enable All Saints, Bloxham, to become a member of the Society in 1896. The School had been founded as early as

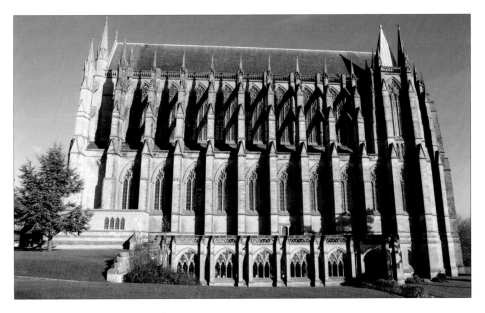

26 *Lancing Chapel. The vast and magnificent chapel is what everyone remembers of Lancing. In Britain only Westminster Abbey, York Minster and Liverpool Cathedral are higher. Dramatic and splendid, it was Woodard's project and proved to be a bottomless pit, not least in diverting funds from essential building for his other schools.*

1860 for 'the education of the sons of tradesmen, farmers, clerks and others of the middle class'. Soon after it opened it was offered to Woodard for £5,000. He turned it down and it was taken on instead by a Fellow of New College, P.R. Egerton. He made a success of it and on several occasions tried to persuade Woodard to take it on and incorporate it into his family of schools. Woodard, however, was pre-occupied in his later years and considered Bloxham a bridge too far. It was not until after his death that, in 1896, and with 180 pupils, it was incorporated into the Woodard family.

It was W.H. Auden who said: 'The first condition for a successful school is a beautiful situation.' Woodard took great care in choosing stunning locations for all his new foundations. In addition he once wrote: 'No system of education would be perfect which did not provide for the cultivation of the pupils through the agency of the highest examples of architecture.' And in this he chose as his chief lieutenant, Richard Carpenter who planned Lancing and Hurstpierpoint, and saw through the building of the latter before his untimely death in 1854. He was succeeded by his son, Herbert, ably supported by his partners Slater and Ingelow, who was responsible for all the subsequent key buildings in the Southern and Midland schools until his death in 1893. Sir Nikolaus Pevsner's series on 'The Buildings of England' can be regarded as the ultimate authority on building design. Here he writes about Lancing:

> High up on a beautiful exposed site above the Adur. Some atonement for the many heaps of ugliness which the 19th century uploaded blindly on the English landscape. The huge chapel is what everyone will remember, but the school buildings are just as good in their quieter way. Halfway up the drive, chapel and quadrangle suddenly compose so perfectly that the elusive dream of the Gothic Revival suddenly seems to be a possibility. This is nearer to Pugin's vision than any of his own buildings.

> Woodard was lucky in his architect: R.C. Carpenter, whom he had met whilst working at Bethnal Green, was almost the only person in England who could design Gothic buildings with the right mixtures of competence, sincerity and common sense. Pugin and Butterfield would have been too fanatical, the rank-and-file would not have cared enough … more than anyone else he could have made the Gothic Revival work but he died too young. His death at 45 was as great a loss as Pugin's.

The Carpenters were well chosen and, as we have seen, were concurrently directly involved in the great wave of Anglican High Church building in Brighton, orchestrated by the Wagner family. Carpenters, Wagners and Woodards were all fully committed members of the Gothic Revival. Dating from the 1830s, driven

27   *Lancing Chapel interior. To the glory of God and the spiritual heart of the Woodard family of schools.*

28 *Ardingly Chapel. Built by Herbert Carpenter and his partner William Slater it was completed in 1883, '... tall and ambitious ... it is a noble piece for a school chapel,' says Pevsner.*

by its high priest Pugin, it was attempting to recreate a medieval and above all what was seen as a Catholic world. Pointed arches and flying buttresses were its characteristics and it became the house style of High Victorian Britain, driven along on a tide of vigorous and revived Christianity.

Woodard was determined that the chapels in all his schools should be grand and dominating in scale and appearance. They should be seen from afar as the very heart of the school and as symbolic Gospel beacons on the hilltops. It should not be forgotten, however, that, as we have already seen at Lancing, grand architectural schemes have equally grand economics.

His chapels, of course, were equipped for the ceremonial dimension to the Anglo-Catholic worship which was so fundamental to a Woodard education – full morning and evening service, a Communion service with sermon on Sundays and Saints days, coloured altar fronts, bowing towards the altar, candles at the altar, flowers, the use of cassocks and surplices, and beautiful plainsong music. These are what made Woodard's schools distinctive and unusual.

Although in many respects conservative and traditional in his thinking, Woodard was also a practical man who was not afraid to adopt the innovations of others, for example, with the concept of monitors, servitors, and a training college for teachers. He grappled with the problems of the day, and tried to resolve them with practical solutions. It was his friend Archdeacon Hare who wrote to him: 'You in common with most men of practical energy – with the Duke of Wellington, for example, and with Bonaparte – have a special gift of seeing all things with intensity from your point of view and overlooking or discharging all difficulties and objections.' There are, of course, both strengths and weaknesses in these characteristics: the former enabled him to accomplish great things, the latter prevented him from achieving what he set out to do. Perhaps in the end, and especially after 1870, his rigidity, narrowness and dogmatism held the Society back.

Woodard, too, makes an interesting contrast with Cardinal Newman. Both were products of the Tractarian movement at Oxford. Newman's one foundation (the Catholic University in Dublin) was a failure: his seminal book *The Idea of a University* was intellectually way beyond anything Woodard could do. Newman was a philosopher, Woodard a practical administrator. Newman was the finished product of Trinity and Oriel, Woodard had no more than a pass degree. His contribution was in bricks and mortar rather than in inspiration. Woodard was an entrepreneur who got things done, Newman was a visionary with a masterly literary style who raised people's horizons. Ultimately, of course, the difference between the two lay in the fact that Newman left the Church of England to become a Roman Catholic. The flight to Rome was a hugely public and controversial issue in the Church of England at this time. In fact they complemented each other in providing a strong educational dimension to the enthusiasm, vigour and drive of the Oxford Movement.

A defining measure of a school is the contribution to life and society of its former pupils. In 1895 the *Hurst Johnian Magazine* published the results of a survey it had undertaken on the professions of some of the boys who had left the School since its foundation 46 years earlier:

- 127 had gone into the ministry of the Church of England, eight of them were Cathedral canons or above, and there were senior churchmen in New Zealand, South Africa and Canada. A number of these were missionaries, some of them serving in the Universities Mission to Central Africa which had been founded by Oxford, Cambridge, Dublin and Durham in 1858. Collectively the contribution of these products of a Woodard school to the growth of the Anglican Church was enormous.
- 80 were schoolmasters, half of whom had taught in a Woodard school at some stage of their career, nine had become headmasters in places as diverse as Australia, New Zealand, South Africa, Hong Kong and Hawaii.
- 70 were in medicine, dentistry and agricultural science.
- 80 were in military service, including four major generals, and nine lieutenant colonels.

These examples and figures from just one school provide more than enough justification for Woodard's foundation of schools for service to the wider community, at home and abroad, and to foster in a selfless way all that was best in the British Empire.

TEN

Woodard Post-Woodard

When Nathaniel Woodard died in 1891 his job was half done. Throughout his life he had been driven by a sense of mission. The re-establishment of the Church of England at the heart of the nation through the vehicle of a network of schools was his vocation; his entrepreneurial spirit the means by which it could all be made to happen.

He left his 10 schools and the Society of St Nicolas in a precarious position. And yet now, 120 years after his death, the family has grown to 45 member schools, and in many respects his fundamental aims have been more than fulfilled though not always in ways which he would have expected or even recognised. Times change, however, and aims and ambitions are re-assessed and re-interpreted.

By the end of the 19th century, some elements in the High Church party of the Church of England were less involved in the philosophy and business of education, and were putting overmuch emphasis on the government of the Church, its ceremony, ritual and liturgy, its buildings and intellectual life. Its critics would say that some of the early reforming vigour of the Oxford Movement had dissipated and ebbed away. There was, and is, however, a noble tradition of High Church parishes serving the poorest parts of the great cities, Liverpool and in parts of London, for example. In this spirit several of the Woodard schools founded missions in the midst of urban deprivation.

The Camberwell Mission, founded by Lancing, providing a youth club and a variety of social and welfare facilities, has served its community well. It was established in 1909 in the slum parish of St John the Divine, Kennington. Here 6,000 people inhabited an area of 17 acres, a territory scheduled by General William Booth in his classic survey of London's Poor as 'a haunt of criminals and centre of poverty'.

These close links survive to this day and are epitomised in the story of a Camberwell resident David Quarty who won a boarding scholarship to

Hurstpierpoint College, went on to Lancing where he became Head Boy and has now returned to Camberwell to teach at St Michael and All Angels Academy, which opened in 2008 to replace the Archbishop Michael Ramsey School.

In addition Ardingly founded and financed a vibrant Mission Centre with a gymnasium, club room, canteen and library in Poplar in 1922. Its purpose was 'to keep local boys and men off the streets and to train them to be good and useful citizens as well as faithful members of the Church'. It flourished, and there were close links between the College and this community, until it was destroyed by German bombs in 1940. There has always been a strong sense of community in and around the Woodard schools.

However these school communities were sorely tested as they coped as best they could with the trials, tribulations and tragedies of the First World War. Most of the younger teachers left for the Front, basic provisions were in short supply, playing fields were dug up in order to grow vegetables, and the casualty lists were unceasing. At Ardingly 146 out of 1,200 old boys who served were killed, 108 Hurst Johnians lost their lives, and 81 of the 270 boys at Lancing in 1914 had been killed in action by 1918. To us today these figures are beyond comprehension.

When it was over the schools struggled with the post-War inflation, and then, after a brief respite in the later 1920s, with the depression of the early 1930s.

Following the departure of the Woodard 'old guard' at the end of the 19th and beginning of the 20th centuries, fresh blood was desperately needed in the Society. In some measure this was provided in the form of Lyttelton, Bishop of Southampton, who succeeded Lowe as Provost of Lancing; and Southwell, Provost from 1903-16, and again 1926-37. Importantly it was Southwell who ensured that Woodard's draft statutes dating from 1848 were brought up to date and re-formed in 1934. Kenneth Kirk, Bishop of Oxford, and Provost from 1937-43, developed further this process of modernisation by appointing a Society bursar at £1,000 p.a. These were men who were capable of grasping nettles and could see the need for change if the schools were to survive and indeed grow.

Throughout this period there was competition from the State as it set up its own grammar schools (491 in 1904 to 1616 in 1925) which had very low fees and many free places, and also for a brief period from the energetic figure of Percy Warrington, Secretary of the Church of England Trust, an evangelical group determined to curb the growth of the Woodard schools and also the Roman Catholic Church. He set out to establish a chain of evangelical public schools. Starting with the purchase of Wellington School in Shropshire in 1920 which was turned into Wrekin College, he aimed to finance these schools on borrowed money, using the equity in one school as security for the next. High death duties and declining income from farming saw a number of country houses come on to the market, and both Canford and Stowe (with a head, the renowned J.F. Roxburgh, recruited from Lancing) were opened on the same day in 1923. By 1932, however, as the recession bit, it was clear that Warrington had over-stretched himself, and his creditors demanded the resignation of both himself and his governors as the price of further financial support. The immediate threat to the Woodard schools of the evangelical revolution was over.

There were challenges, too, in the Second World War. Lancing hosted Westminster School at the time of the Munich Crisis when war was expected at any moment, and then was evacuated via Ellesmere and Denstone to Shropshire where it remained for the next six years. Meanwhile its buildings played a notable and valuable role in the war effort as part of HMS *King Alfred*, a training base for naval officers. Ardingly and Hurstpierpoint took the bold decision to stay put as invasion threatened the south-east of England. Their courage was rewarded and despite some privations their numbers held up well throughout the war years, not least because Eastbourne College and Brighton College, as well as Lancing, were all evacuated.

Butler's Education Act of 1944 and the Fleming Commission on *The Future of the Public Schools* did not augur well for the independent sector. The former re-organised secondary education and in particular the grammar schools which, excepting the direct grant schools, were no longer allowed to charge fees. The State was now providing free grammar school education in every town in the land and this would assuredly be attractive to parents who previously felt that they had to pay for their children to attend private boarding schools in order to get a decent education. The Fleming Commission recommended that 25 per cent of all places in the public schools should be free. This would wreak havoc with the finances of the cheaper schools such as those in the Woodard family.

As Britain emerged from war into what became known as the Age of Austerity, no one would have been hugely surprised if Woodard's schools had quietly slipped away exactly one hundred years after his grand design had been launched.

Fortunately the last 60 years have seen steady and sustained growth, and now as the 200th anniversary of the birth of the Founder approaches, the Woodard schools are in a notably stronger position than they have ever been. There are 45 schools with 30,000 pupils, 50,000 parents (allowing for siblings), 3,000 teachers and an equal number of support staff, plus 750 governors. This is an organisation of considerable significance in the national educational landscape. What has caused this revolution in fortunes in the past 60 years?

First and foremost, there has been substantial economic growth which has favoured all independent schools which have been prepared to help themselves. There have been temporary hiccups – inflation in the late '60s and early '70s; recession 1979-81, 1990-91 and again 2008-10; but these have been short-term set backs in a period of long-term growing prosperity. For independent schools the state of the economy, and therefore parents' ability to pay fees, is a defining feature.

It should be noted also that independent schools have done at least as well under Labour governments as they have under those of the generally more friendly Conservatives. The ending of selection in the State system, and in particular the abolition of the direct grant schools in 1976, drove many parents away from the State into the independent sector. It has to be said that all the Woodard fee-paying secondary schools have benefited from the disappearance of the local State grammar school.

Second, a series of strong headmasters supported by astute governors, has enabled the schools to take advantage of the opportunities put before them. Canon Ronald Howard at Hurstpierpoint (267 boys when he arrived in 1945 to 462 when he retired in 1964) and Canon George Snow at Ardingly raised numbers, and also fees, to transform their schools. Ian Beer at Ellesmere (1962-69) and then at Lancing (1969-81) was an important and influential figure in the independent school world and so far the only Woodard head to have been Chairman of HMC (the Headmasters' and Headmistresses' Conference). Importantly heads and governors were given the scope and independence to run their schools as they thought fit, without undue interference from the Society. Heads were appointed by governors on grounds of their professional competence, not solely because of the hue and colour of their clerical cloth.

Often it is said that it is heads who make schools. Actually the most fundamental component of any school is its governing body. Wise, committed and attentive governors will appoint good heads and then support them. Crucially they will also remove heads who, for whatever reason, are not up to the job. The Woodard schools have been sensibly governed by boards which have been well balanced between clergymen and laymen with the appropriate professional skills. Mostly they have managed to respect their past, but importantly they have never taken their eye off the market place. And in this regard they have been adaptable. At the end of the Second World War most Woodard schools were boarding schools for boys, aged 13-18. In a competitive and rapidly changing market place to have remained thus would have meant death. Today most are co-educational, embrace the full age range from three to 18, and when boarding has been retained it has been flexible in nature with a strong international dimension.

Third, a clear and unapologetically Christian, and still High Church Anglican, ethos has made many of the Woodard schools distinctive. In a half century in which society has become increasingly secular, the Woodard schools have stuck firmly to their principles. These Christian beliefs and values have underpinned and permeated all that each school has striven to undertake and achieve.

It is characteristic of this vision and ethos that schools set out to inculcate the importance of the value of love, forgiveness, truthfulness, integrity, courage, generosity and respect for all people. Allied to this is the view that education in a

Woodard school is more than simply a service industry in teaching and learning skills, important though these are, but that it also involves the inculcation of a wider view of life, working to change the world for the better, pursuing justice and peace.

It is important also to note that the fee-paying schools have established a number of bursaries in order to open themselves to pupils from poorer and disadvantaged families, exactly mirroring the original aims of the Founder.

Although the schools seek to provide experience of Anglican Christian worship, and particularly the role of the Eucharist, they do not set out to evangelise, nor do they embrace extreme views; and just for the record pupils are not expected to go to confession either! The schools are not oppressively or overly-religious but an aura of Christianity does pervade. They celebrate religious, cultural and ethnic diversity, and they encourage dialogue and understanding. They look for what unites people, not what divides them. Although Woodard himself was narrowly focused, his successors have forged a Christianity which is not frightened to change. There has been a sturdy appreciation of the society in which it finds itself and functions. In an age when the connection between religion and education is controversial and often misunderstood, the Woodard schools hold firmly to their beliefs and values.

Chaplains still play a significant role in the Woodard schools, not only pastorally and as teachers, but also in formulating ethos and character. This is described further in the Appendix. It is wholly in the spirit of the Founder that the Corporation is organising a national conference at Liverpool Hope University in the summer of 2011 to reflect on the role of school chaplaincy in the 21st century.

The Woodard Corporation is the formal organisation with its headquarters at Abbots Bromley School for Girls, which co-ordinates, oversees and serves this family of 45 schools – 22 owned, 15 affiliated and eight associated – belonging to both maintained and independent sectors, selective and non-selective, preparatory, senior, day, boarding, co-educational, single sex, and now academies. Collectively the family contains an unrivalled range of knowledge of education in England, and significantly it is one of the very few organisations which has members in both the independent and maintained sectors of education.

It would be fair to say that the structure and workings of the Corporation, and its predecessor the Society of St Nicolas, have not always been straightforward. Woodard's autocratic style was incompatible with an effective and decentralised structure. Established in 1848, with Woodard at its centre as Provost until he died in 1891, his draft statutes were not completed in his lifetime. Reform could not really get underway until the conservative Edward Lowe retired from the post of Provost in 1898. Gradually thereafter some change was made and the statutes were finally completed in 1934. This basic constitution remained until 2004 when it was re-configured.

At the heart of this family of schools, the Corporation has three funda-mental purposes:

1.   A link between schools – sharing best practice, providing a clear bridge, not least between the maintained and independent sectors; the former, for example, bringing its insights and expertise in the pedagogy of teaching and learning, the latter its commitment and experience in pastoral care and very rich extra-curricular provision. It is a meeting place, a forum for those directly involved in the educational process. As teacher training becomes less institutional and more school based, groups of schools, such as Woodard, with their wide range of members will have a major role to play in the professional training and development of teachers. This, of course, is where the Founder started in establishing a facility for training teachers on the job at Hurstpierpoint College in 1853, leading to the qualification of Associate of the Society of St Nicolas. It provides, too, a focus for leadership training and succession planning, identifying within the family youthful talent and then providing the opportunity for its development so that there is a steady stream of leaders of the Woodard schools in the years ahead. It is notable how many Woodard heads in the early years came from within the family. Succession planning is not a new concept. The increasing complexities of school management have however made it even more important.

29   *Lancing Prep School at Mowden. Edwardian calm in Hove. Three generations of the Snell family owned and ran the Mowden School until it was incorporated into the Woodard family in 2002 as the prep school of Lancing College.*

2.   The development of the Woodard brand name – to the benefit of all members of the family. The Woodard schools have a reputation for good academic standards, supportive pastoral care and a wide range of extra-curricular activities. And they are also known for their Christian, and especially Anglican ethos. Few parents today would choose a Woodard school for their children solely for this reason; many, however, like the strong spiritual dimension to life, the Christian aura, an atmosphere that is not solely secular.

3.   Extending schools and in particular academies – creating good schools where they were lacking is what Nathaniel Woodard did. In the last decade the family has grown fast from 32 schools in 2000 to 45 today, and in particular the involvement in the government's Academies programme has been directly in the Founder's tradition. The Corporation has the resources, energy and expertise to further this important work from the centre. It should be noted, however, that it is the State, supported by an independent and separate trust, which is financing this programme.

Inevitably in any such organisation there will be tensions between the centre and the individual school units in the regions. The schools are rightly concerned with the efficient and effective day-to-day running of their own individual and unique communities. The centre with its view over the whole Corporation seeks to hold the family together, develop the interests of all of its members and take on board newcomers. Nathaniel Woodard left no endowments and so the services provided by the centre have to be financed by levies on the owned member schools.

Unlike the City Livery companies where charitable endowments are centrally held and schools have been spawned from the centre, the Woodard Corporation has grown from the outside, often in an apparently haphazard manner.

It is worth keeping all this in mind when considering how most effectively a modern organisation can be structured so that it serves the interests of all of its members. Trying to be all things to all men has rarely proved a fruitful policy.

Nathaniel Woodard set out to provide opportunities for young people, to create good schools where they were markedly lacking. In 2004 New Labour had exactly the same aim when it launched the City Academies movement. Academies were designed not for one specific economic or social group but rather to replace schools which were failing, or to provide new schools where there were none. They were government funded, open to pupils of all abilities, free and run, not by the local education authority, but rather by private sector sponsors in partnership with central government. These sponsorships came from charities, churches, universities, philanthropic businessmen, City Livery companies, and leading independent schools, collectively people and institutions of good standing in the community. Through the governing body they provided the vision, expertise and experience

30, 31 & 32 *The Littlehampton Academy. The architect's drawings of the front of the new building … of the main atrium … and aerial view.*

in running the school, setting its strategic priorities and appointing the principal. They set out to provide an outstanding and innovatory education with the aid of a state-of -the-art new building to enable young people to play a full part in life as it is at the outset of the 21st century. Academies are beacons of hope for the young people who, by and large, have not been well served by the education system.

This was the opportunity for the Woodard Corporation to extend its work into new but familiar territory, to use all of its accumulated knowledge and experience of how schools work, to help build new ones. With nice historical symmetry, the first two were a stone's throw from Shoreham, in the town of Littlehampton and village of Lancing. The Littlehampton Academy was created to replace Littlehampton Community School and opened in September 2009, whilst in Lancing village, the Sir Robert Woodard Academy (named after the great-grandson of the Founder) replaced the Boundstone Community College.

It is hoped to open two more in 2011. The Woodard Academy in Maidstone will replace the Astor of Hever School with its own 'new build' ready for 2014. Its published ethos is based on the Christian values of respect, loyalty and truth, trust and integrity. At the same time, reflecting modern-day society, it welcomes people of all faiths and of none, and it sets out openly to encourage understanding, diversity and tolerance for all. Meanwhile in Stoke-on-Trent, Woodard has gone into partnership with the Diocese of Lichfield to merge two schools (Berry Hill and St Peter's High School) into one, St Peter's Academy. Its distinctive Christian character will be demonstrated by service to the community, the promotion of spiritual and moral values, and a commitment to community cohesion. This is an important venture in the city of Stoke which has suffered so much deprivation as a result of the economic process of de-industrialisation. To have a magnificent and stunning new educational building at the heart of this regeneration of a once proud city is important and sends out a very clear message.

Interestingly, too, the Corporation will work closely with Keele and Manchester Metropolitan universities to establish St Peter's Academy as a centre of excellence for teacher development – developing a culture of continuous improvement, offering all staff the opportunity to improve professional and personal skills. This is an exact throwback to the setting up by Woodard of a teacher training establishment at Hurstpierpoint in 1853, providing a training course for young teachers. Then and now Woodard is a forum for professional development.

Now, of course, the Coalition government which came into power in May 2010 has embraced, and indeed expanded in range, the New Labour Academy concept for all maintained schools. It seeks to give schools the freedom to run their communities as they think best meets the needs of the pupils. Again, this philosophy is absolutely in the spirit and tradition of the Founder. The Academies movement is seen by its supporters as one of the most exciting, and important, educational initiatives in this country for a very long time. It brings to full circle the work which Nathaniel Woodard founded.

In the early 1940s the young Sir John Keegan, one of Britain's greatest military historians, was a boy at King's College, Taunton. Sixty years later he wrote about his schooldays:

> I suppose it should be called ethos. King's was not a grand school. It did not aspire to compete with Eton or Winchester or even Marlborough. It was informed, nevertheless, by the gentlemanly Christian ethic, then the admired national norm, determining good behaviour and still not entirely extirpated even in these days of *Men Behaving Badly* and football yobbery. The norm was extremely powerful. Big boys were protective of small boys. Small boys were nice to each other. Not only was there no bullying; the atmosphere at the school, between staff and boys, and between boys, of whatever age, was friendly and co-operative. There was respect for learning. Games though important, were not a fetish. The spirit was, I suppose, exactly what Canon Woodard wished in the school he founded – scholarly, Christian, humanistic.

That special ethos pervades the Woodard schools today and reflects the remarkable vision and energy of the Founder, Nathaniel Woodard. We can be immensely proud of the important legacy of good schools which he left and which is being continued in the new academy schools being established for the 21st century. All those who have ever been involved in his family of schools as governors, staff, parents and above all, pupils, will have good cause to celebrate his 200th birthday on 21 March 2011.

APPENDIX

The Woodard Schools Today

What does it actually mean to be a Woodard school today? This was the final question which needed to be answered in my journey in search of Nathaniel Woodard and the world he has created.

Each school was asked three fundamental questions:

1. What is the nature and character of your school today?
2. How did it become involved in the Woodard family?
3. What does this mean to the school today?

This is what they said:

ABBOTS BROMLEY SCHOOL FOR GIRLS

STAFFORDSHIRE

Peter Green, Chaplain. Julie Dowling, Head

1. Abbots Bromley is a small, independent girls' school at the secondary level and which, with Roch House (a mixed Preparatory School and an integral part of A.B.), remains an incorporated member of the Woodard Corporation. It is not academically selective, but enjoys excellent public examination results at both GCSE and A Level with students gaining places at the most prestigious universities in the UK and overseas. Having been historically predominantly a boarding school, numbers are supplemented by day pupils from the local area. In addition to a mainstream academic curriculum, it offers specialist facilities in dancing (the Alkins School of Ballet being an integral part of the school) and equestrianism.

   It is not easy to characterise an institution that one is part of, although new members of staff are struck by the comparative gentleness of the educational ambience. It is traditional without being stuffy and because of its non-selective admissions policy, its pupils are hard to generalise about – from the energetic extroverts to the more reserved, a mixture of aptitudes: academic, sporting, artistic, performing.

2. It is one of the original schools founded by Woodard himself – although he was famously reluctant to found a girls' school, being initially inclined to think it a waste of his time and effort. Despite this, he is still fondly remembered by those most aware of the history.

3. It varies greatly. All girls in Year 7 are taught about the foundation of the school as part of the religious studies syllabus and the weekly Eucharist is very specifically part of our identity as a Woodard school. Because so many of the neighbouring Woodard schools are mixed, its relationship to other elements of the Corporation are not as strong as they have been in the past. However, whilst respecting the religious diversity within the membership of the school, its Anglo-Catholic character and tradition are still much respected.

Head Girl: Hannah Thomas

ROCH HOUSE PREPARATORY SCHOOL

STAFFORDSHIRE

Ann Johnson, Head

Roch House Preparatory School is a small and friendly prep school where each pupil is encouraged to find and develop their talents and appreciate the talents of others.

Roch House was declared a separate school in September 2009 when boys were admitted into the Kindergarten for the first time after enjoying more than 100 years as the girls-only Junior Department of Abbots Bromley School for Girls.

The strong Christian ethos influences every level of interaction. Our pupils are happy, confident and show great empathy towards each other and the wider world.

ALDERLEY EDGE SCHOOL FOR GIRLS
CHESHIRE
Mary Hostler, Lay Chaplain. Sue Goff, Head

1.   Alderley Edge School for Girls came into being in 1999 when two independent girls' schools, St Hilary's Church of England School and Mount Carmel Roman Catholic Convent, merged. The nature and character of the School today can be summed up as '… an ecumenical community based on mutual respect for those enduring qualities which encourage global citizenship.' (Goff, 2010). The School's vision statement expands on this, stating:

> AESG is … a dynamic school which fosters the wellbeing of each individual within a welcoming, safe and supportive environment. We recognise commitment, hard work and success, setting ourselves aspirational challenges to develop our talents to the full …. We are proud of our school and its Christian values, yet respect the beliefs of others in our community. We believe in social justice for all and feel a sense of responsibility for those less fortunate, for whom we provide support both locally and globally through our fundraising and community service.

There are 600 girls in the Junior and Senior schools and a strong pastoral support system, recognised as 'outstanding', operates throughout. The School has a team of four chaplains who support the spiritual awareness and development of girls and staff within the School. The part-time RC Lay Chaplain co-ordinates the chaplaincy team which includes a RC priest, Church of England priest (designated as the Woodard Chaplain) and a Methodist minister.

2. St Hilary's Girls' School joined the Woodard Corporation in 1955. Miss Helena Adcock and Miss Doris Gliddon had taken over as joint principals and owners of the School in 1927. In 1950 they appointed Miss Ethel Dawson as Headmistress. The two ladies were concerned to secure the Christian tradition of the School so they transferred ownership of the School to the Woodard Corporation on 18 October 1955. The Misses Adcock and Gliddon joined the Governors, posts which they held for a further 21 years. The School was dedicated into the family of Woodard at a service in Chester. An ex-pupil of St Hilary's remembers that 'the girls were always treated as individuals and not part of a crowd and Christian values and worship were promoted.' AESG is now an associated Woodard school.

3. For AESG today, association with Woodard is maintained because of the congruence between the educational principles and practice within the School and the reputation of Woodard for its promotion of 'faith, unity and vision'. As in all Woodard schools, the Christian ethos is fundamental to AESG, and parents seeking more than academic excellence, who want to be assured that their daughter will receive individual interest, be valued whatever faith they hold, and where pastoral care and a holistic approach to education have a high priority, are reassured when they can see that the Head and Governors hold to the values and vision of the Woodard schools.

Head Girl: Cerys Owens

ARCHBISHOP TEMPLE SCHOOL

PRESTON

Adrian Thompson, Chaplain. Mark Jackson, Acting Head

1.   Archbishop Temple School is an 11-16 Church of England Technology and Humanities College. Our Church of England foundation ensures that the traditional Christian values of respect, tolerance, honesty, compassion, humility, self-discipline and good manners, are paired with the aspirations of a high attaining faith school. We welcome families of other world faiths and believe the School is richer for the spiritual and cultural diversity that this brings. The Christian *faith* encourages us to show our love for God and one another through acts of *service*. Our sharing of Christian values, celebrations and acts of service, within our daily lives at Archbishop Temple School, helps *nurture* a community in which God's love is made visible. The essence of this vision for the life of our School is captured in our mission statement and motto:

Nurturing a living Christian community through
lives of learning, worship and service
'Whoever serves me must follow me; and where I am, my servant also will be.' John 12, 26

FAITH + NURTURE + SERVICE

2.   The Headteacher was invited to join the Woodard Foundation during 2009.

3.   Our school is a very new addition to the Woodard family, but we already enjoyed taking the whole of our Year 7 to Blackburn Cathedral to join with pupils from other Woodard Schools in a communion service of worship, prayer and celebration, during which we were welcomed into the Woodard Foundation. We look forward to discerning how this new relationship will develop in the years ahead.

Head Boy: Daniel Bayliss
Head Girl: Alice Wright

ARDINGLY COLLEGE

HAYWARDS HEATH, WEST SUSSEX

David Lawrence-March, Chaplain. Peter Green, Head.
Chris Calvey, Prep Head

Ardingly College, one of the three original Woodard schools, takes its maintenance of the Woodard ethos as a central pillar of its foundation. The College states that, as a Woodard school, we are first and foremost a Eucharistic Community, in which every member of the College is encouraged, as far as their conscience allows, to meet with Jesus in the Bread and Wine of the Altar.

The daily celebration of the Eucharist is at the heart of our proclamation of the Woodard ethos. We are fortunate in having not one but two chapels: the Chapel of St Saviour (the original nomenclature of the College) and the Crypt Chapel of the Ascension, and both are seen and used as key locations within the College.

The Chapel of St Saviour is used for the full school celebrations: the College Mass (for the Senior School) on Wednesdays and the Prep School Mass on Fridays. Both of these are full sung solemn celebrations with many students taking part as altar servers, readers, ushers and musicians. It is also the venue for assemblies and other special services, including weddings and baptisms for Old Ardinians.

The Crypt Chapel of the Ascension, where the Blessed Sacrament is reserved, is used for the daily Mass on other days, including Sundays. It is also used for House Chapel services on a rota basis on weekday mornings, for First Communion and Confirmation classes, for the daily Office on weekdays, and is open from early in the morning until the evening as a place for prayer and as a 'quiet place'. It is also used for frequent celebrations of the Eucharist during holiday time if the Chaplain, who lives on site, is in residence and not involved in services in local parishes.

Each house, boarding and day, has a House Sacristan who co-ordinates with the School Sacristans when his or her house is 'duty house' at the College Mass. There is a similar system in the Prep School, with a regular team of boys and girls involved in their celebration on Fridays.

The Senior Sacristan is an Upper Sixth form student with prefectorial status, who is assisted by a Deputy Sacristan and other School Sacristans, both senior and junior students, who provide the core group of servers at the College Mass and who, between them, provide readers and servers at the celebrations in the Crypt Chapel. The Senior and Deputy Sacristans are also Eucharistic Ministers, together with a group of five members of staff.

The Christian Union meets weekly, co-ordinated by a member of staff, who is also a Eucharistic Minister, and has a diverse membership across all groups and traditions. There are also staff and parental prayer groups that meet regularly.

Each year students from both Senior and Prep Schools are prepared for Confirmation (and, if necessary, for Baptism), and pupils in Years 5 and 6 may also be prepared for First Holy Communion.

Head Boy: Valentin Seeger
Head Girl: Katherine Harris

THE BISHOP OF HEREFORD'S BLUECOAT SCHOOL
HEREFORD
Sara Catlow-Hawkins, Headteacher

At Bishop's we aim to be a 'vibrant Christian learning community' enabling students to flourish academically and socially. Our responsibility is to recognise the very best each student can do and to work to ensure the very best outcome.

Schools are more than buildings and the quality of a school can be judged on the quality of relationships between students and staff, the involvement and achievement of students and the quality of their contribution to the community. In addition to the formal curriculum there are lots of opportunities for young people to develop their many gifts and talents, contribute to school life and broaden their experiences. Students develop self-reliance, confidence and adaptability and are able to take on responsibilities according to their interests, ranging from being part of our Student Council, helping in the Library or providing audio visual support for productions to leading teams and performing.

We value our reputation as a happy, caring community where students are encouraged to take responsibility for their own learning and development. It is important that they feel supported during their life at school so each student belongs to a house. Our house structure ensures each young person is nurtured in their school life through belonging to their tutor group. Leadership is particularly valued and many Year 11 students will apply for, and be successful as, School Prefects and Listeners. We also offer a full programme of educational visits which enrich and extend learning in the classroom.

Around the turn of the 1980s the Woodard Corporation began a policy of offering affiliated status to some CE Aided Schools as part of what we would now call their inclusion policy. The Provost of Woodard (Keith Wilkes) came to see our Diocescan Director of Education, then Christopher Herbert, and together they came to see me.

It struck a chord with me as I had worked for four years full-time for The Bloxham Project, an enquiry into the Christian faith and values of Church independent boarding schools. During this I had got to know Woodard Schools and worked with several of them. I could see that if we joined with them,

a) making common cause with a group of avowedly Christian schools would allow Bishop's to show where it stood as a church school. It did.
b) we would have something to offer them from the State sector
c) it could enhance Bishop's profile by extending our collaboration with other schools and we would learn from each other.

In my time the only other school to have the same status was Archbishop Ramsey's School in London.

(John Chapman, Headteacher at the time of affiliation)

Head Boy: Ed Rawcliffe
Head Girl: Beth Bird

BISHOP STOPFORD SCHOOL
KETTERING, NORTHAMPTONSHIRE
Jill Silverthorne, Assistant Head. Margaret Holman, Head

1. Bishop Stopford School is an 11-18 mixed school, based in Kettering, Northamptonshire. With more than 1,400 students (over 350 in the sixth form), it is a thriving educational community with core values of 'Faith', 'Justice', 'Truth', 'Responsibility' and 'Compassion'. Students travel from across the county and beyond to attend the school. The most recent Ofsted report grades the school as 'Outstanding', praising its academic achievements, leadership and management, and quality of care, amongst other areas. Whilst being a Technology College, Bishop Stopford School prides itself on all round achievements: sports and arts are as high achieving as the technology subjects.

    There is a thriving enrichment programme, and a long-established tradition of off-site learning. This includes visits to the Scilly Isles or Hawaii, international sports tours, participation in national competitions in the arts and other areas.

    The role of the sixth form is significant in school, and there is a strong tradition of sixth formers supporting students in Years 7-11. They are trained to teach parts of the curriculum, mentor and provide a range of enrichment activities for younger students.

    Bishop Stopford School is well recognised for its innovative approach to the curriculum. It is the first school in the country to have a sustainability curriculum at Key Stage 3 in which all students participate, and the first school to provide a business curriculum in Logistics at Key Stage 4. Approaches to Continuing Professional Development, coaching and partnership work with other schools and industry are highly regarded.

2. The School became part of the Woodard family because of the striking similarities in both organisations' ethos and values. Bishop Stopford's leadership team was looking to work with organisations which were supportive of its ethos, and, crucially, which would bring added value. The Woodard family of schools by its very nature would extend capacity and give a national framework, and this has proved invaluable over the years. The Church of England link was also an essential reason for being involved.

3. The School has benefited enormously from belonging to the Woodard family. There has been a range of provision which we have enjoyed, from Prefects' Courses, the annual Masterclasses at Trinity and Chaplains' Conferences, as well as benefiting from networking with other Woodard heads. The School has also been happy to reciprocate by providing a tutor for the Masterclasses. The sense of tradition has been much appreciated, and, more recently, the opportunity to be challenged by the Woodard family in our strategic thinking and contributions. We have enjoyed visits from those employed at Woodard – both in terms of chaplaincy work and for strategic discussions. We are happy to honour the founding father – and value being members of this unique family, coupling traditional values with a forward thinking approach.

Head Boy: Alex Coleman
Head Girl: Katherine Ingham

THE BISHOPS' BLUE COAT CHURCH OF ENGLAND HIGH SCHOOL CHESTER
Paul North, Chaplain. Justin Blakebrough, Head

1. The Bishops' Bluecoat Church of England High School, Chester is a co-educational school with just more than 1,000 pupils aged from 11 to 19. Drawing its students from the immediate locality, as well as from several neighbouring local authorities, Bishops' has a diverse cohort with a wide range of church backgrounds and many with none at all. The responsibility of using opportunities for both mission and nurture is one which the chaplain and many staff consider to be very important. There is strength in the many different worship styles within the School. In the local area Bishops' is known as a popular, high achieving, caring school with a strong Christian ethos where pupils are valued and supported in all areas of life.

2. When Bishops' became a Woodard school it was the only Anglican church school in the local authority. At that time the Bishop, Alan Chesters, a very supportive and active governor, was well acquainted with the Woodard family of schools and suggested that it would be beneficial for the School to join for the support and fellowship that Woodard would provide.

3. This support has been seen in the links with other schools in the region with a marvellous joint Easter project. The extra support in prayer is obviously invaluable to us, knowing we have fellow schools praying for us gives us confidence to serve the Lord, our pupils and community.

Head Girl: Emily Grader
Head Boy: Daniel Allanson

BLOXHAM SCHOOL

BANBURY, OXFORDSHIRE

Michael Price, Chaplain. Mark Allbrook, Head

1.   Bloxham is a mixed boarding school for 11- to 18-year-olds.
About fifty-five per cent of pupils board and most of the day
pupils stay until 9 p.m. every night. There are 430 pupils in all, including 75 pupils in the
'Lower School' which covers Year 7 and 8 children. In the rest of the School the pupils
will be resident in one of the six boarding houses, where day pupils and boarders are
mixed. Most pupils live within one hour's drive of the School and there is a lot of parent
involvement in its day to day life.

Bloxham sees itself as a mildly selective school which has high aspirations for
its pupils. It has a strong tradition of educational support for pupils with dyslexia. It
has its own dyslexia unit. There has been considerable concentration upon academic
achievement in recent years: the opening of a beautiful new library and the major
investment in laptops for pupils is testimony to this.

Bloxham has traditionally focused upon a strong sense of pastoral care and the
spiritual development of all its pupils. The chapel remains at the centre of school life,
just as the founder always intended it to be. It has a long record of excellence in sporting
achievement whether that is in major team sports such as rugby and hockey or in more
specialised activities such as clay pigeon shooting and equestrian events.

2. Philip Egerton, the founder of Bloxham School, was closely allied to many of the
leaders of the Oxford Movement. Bishop Samuel Wilberforce acted as his mentor
and encouraged him in the founding of Bloxham in 1860. When Egerton became an
old man he was eager that the Anglican principles and strong Christian ethos of his
school would remain and so he passed the School into the care of the Woodard family
in 1896.

3. Bloxham is a Eucharistic community in which all share weekly in this central act of
Christian worship. Every member of the School understands the continual thankfulness
for the gifts of creation and salvation that are expressed in the Eucharist. The School
understands itself to be a holy communion in which all care for one another. It believes
itself to be people of the Mass, in which all are sent out in the name of Christ to share
the gifts that we have been given within the Bloxham community.

Head Boy: Elliott Dickinson
Head Girl: Holly Morgan

THE CATHEDRAL SCHOOL

LLANDAFF, CARDIFF

Stephen Morris, Headmaster

The Cathedral School was refounded by Dean Charles Vaughan
in 1880 as a small boys' choir school to support the choral worship
of Llandaff Cathedral. It continued in this vein until the Second World War, when the
Cathedral was bombed. Difficult days followed and, in 1957, the Cathedral asked the
Woodard Corporation to take responsibility for the School. At this time it numbered 190
boys. In 1958 it moved to a new campus, the site of the old bishop's palace in Llandaff,
a much larger site which offered scope for a much better delivery of education and for

future expansion. In 1980 the School became co-educational, and in 1997 ceased to be a boarding school.

The School today numbers 650, boys and girls, aged three to 16; it is planning the introduction of a sixth form within the next few years. The Cathedral choristers continue to be educated here. Every week the school gathers in the Cathedral for a service, and half termly this is a Eucharist. Prayers are offered in chapel daily. Religious education is taught throughout the school, with the teaching of the Christian faith central. The Woodard ethos manifests itself not only in explicit religious observance, but in an ethos of care for each individual child, a heavy emphasis upon the personal, social and moral development of pupils, and an atmosphere of mutual respect and support.

Head Boy: James Groves
Head Girl: Rose Stevens

CROMPTON HOUSE CHURCH OF ENGLAND SCHOOL
OLDHAM

Charles Whitehead, Worship Co-ordinator. Elsie Tough, Head

Founded in 1926, Crompton House was the gift of Miss Crompton and Mrs Ormerod, both members of the Crompton family, to the Church Commissioners for the establishment of a Higher Grade Church school and had an initial intake of 25 pupils. Today it is a Voluntary Aided Anglican 11-18 co-educational Comprehensive school catering for about 1,300 pupils, including a sixth form of 300. It is situated in a pleasant residential area in the Pennine foothills near the border between the Metropolitan Boroughs of Oldham and Rochdale. In recent years the School has grown considerably in numbers from 706 in 1985 to its present position and every year there is considerable over-subscription for the places available. The School has a large catchment area attracting pupils from outside the Oldham Metropolitan Borough from Rochdale, Middleton, Alkrington, Bamford, Littleborough and Saddleworth.

Crompton House is an affiliated Woodard school and our pupils and staff join in events like Master Classes held at Oxford University and Senior Prefects training weekends.

Head Boy: Tom Lowe
Head Girl: Ellis Bradbury

DENSTONE COLLEGE
UTTOXETER, STAFFORDSHIRE

Rupert Jarvis, Chaplain. David Derbyshire, Head

Denstone College, one of Woodard's original schools, was founded in 1868 and opened its doors to pupils for the first time in 1873.

Since its earliest days it has stood literally and metaphorically above the village of Denstone in the Dove Valley that marks the boundary between Staffordshire and Derbyshire. Like a mountain in low-lying ground, it dominates the horizon, and like a cathedral spire it bears witness and points the way both to heaven and to enlightenment. This dual encapsulation – of both educational and spiritual breadth and commitment – is echoed in the College's motto *Lignvm crvcis arbour scientiae*: the wood of the cross is the tree of knowledge.

A statue of Woodard stands in the Lonsdale Quad at the rear of the College, and he would undoubtedly recognise much of what surrounds him. The purpose-built main body of the school is still central to 'the trivial round, the common task', and the route across the Quad past Woodard is heavily used. He may not have been a golf-addict himself, but he would have been delighted to see both pupils and locals making use of the outstanding nine-hole course that lies in front of him.

He would of course be surprised to see so many girls in the College and some so small. Denstone was founded as a boys' school from 13+, but accepted the first girls in 1976. The 211 girls now make up well over a third of its 576 pupils aged 11+. He would also be amazed and enthused by the range and beauty of some of the newer buildings and facilities that have sprung up. The clean modern lines of the Sports Hall and Swimming Pool contrast powerfully with the Gothic Revival style of the main building; the classroom blocks and science labs blend discretely into the overall layout; and the new Roper Building of state-of-the-art teaching facilities and a purpose-built music school shows that the values and standards are traditional, but the impetus and initiative is entirely modern and new: happiness, confidence and achievement underpin the bricks and mortar just as much as the day-to-day life of the College.

He would also be enthused to see his chapel in such regular use, for regular worship, for headmaster's assemblies, and for the pivotal Eucharist in all its forms. He might be surprised at the multimedia screens in the chapel, but not until he had been won over by their flexibility, their discrete installation, and the huge effect they have on the enthusiastic hymn-singing. And he would undoubtedly be delighted to find that the route through the West End of the Chapel was one of the busiest in the College. With its votive stand always aglow with signs of faith and flames of hope, the Ante-Chapel stands at the very fulcrum of the College – a view to the East and the altar of tradition, of serenity, and of worship; and a view to the north and south of what makes the College: pupils demonstrating their happiness, brimming with confidence, and striving for achievement.

Head Boy: Jack Sampson
Head Girl: Georgia Rought Whitta

DERBY HIGH SCHOOL
DERBY
Rachel Barrett, Chaplain. Colin Callaghan, Head

Derby High School educates children from three to 18, with fully co-educational infant and junior sections, from the ages of three to 11 and a senior school for girls only.

The image of the tree of life in the pupil entrance of the senior school reflects the original motto of the school 'Rooted and grounded in love' and reminds us that it is our Christian foundation that gives the school a particular sense of purpose and value. This is a school with a relaxed, happy but purposeful atmosphere where pupils recognise that their best is always good enough.

Founded in 1892 by the Church Schools' Company it came as a shock to the school governing body in the 1950s to discover that the school no longer had any official Church links. It was at this point that a relationship was established with the Woodard Corporation, with the school becoming affiliated to Woodard in 1958. Since 2008 we have been an associated school and it is a connection that we value highly.

As would be expected of a Woodard school, the celebration of the Eucharist plays an important part in shaping our community. This is a particular challenge in our multi-faith context but over the past few years it has been a joy to see the numbers of pupils of other faiths who now choose to receive a blessing alongside those of their Christian peers who receive communion. At our Leavers' Eucharist it is now usual for every member of the U6 who is not a communicant to come forward for a blessing to mark this particular rite of passage.

Our Christian ethos is evident not only in the quality of our worship but also in the quality of our relationships. It is demonstrated practically in the strong commitment to serving others which is a hallmark of our community. As well as raising thousands of pounds for charity each year we also send teams of staff and older pupils to work in orphanages in Thailand or to teach underprivileged children in Ethiopia. Our biennial World Challenge expeditions also include working on a project in the local community.

The Primary department has the Christian ethos as a foundation of everything it does. It embraces the diverse population and the different experiences and religions that the children bring to the school. Parents appreciate this and see it as a strength of their children's personal development at Derby High. We aim to continue to build on this, enhancing the Christian philosophy, strengthening the school chaplaincy and bridging links with visiting clergy and local faith groups.

Junior Head Boy: Pavan Badwal
Junior Head Girl: Niamh Elston

ELLESMERE COLLEGE
ELLESMERE, SHROPSHIRE
David Slim, Chaplain. Brendan Wignall, Head

Ellesmere College was founded by Canon Nathaniel Woodard in 1879 and opened in 1884. It draws stability and strength from membership of the Woodard Corporation which has helped it to establish and promote a unique brand of religious, educational and social traditions.

Influenced by the Christian faith and values that belonging to the Woodard Corporation has helped it to uphold, and using modern educational methods, an Ellesmere education emphasises the importance of the individual and encourages higher aspirations than simply passing examinations. The aim of the College is to produce well-rounded individuals with a sense of purpose who are capable of leading successful, considerate and inspirational lives.

Ellesmere College promotes a positive approach to life in what is now a multicultural community in which respect for Christian values and the contributions of other faiths and cultures help to enrich community life.

Head Boy: Thomas King
Head Girl: Zoe Evans

EXETER CATHEDRAL SCHOOL
EXETER
Carl Turner, Chaplain. Stephen Yeo, Head

1. Exeter Cathedral School is filled with music which lifts the heart. As an ancient choir school nurturing children for life in the 21st century we look to the past with gratitude and forward in hope. As an official *church school* we are pleased to be part of the network of church schools in the Diocese of Exeter and also of the Woodard

Corporation; this means that we mix with independent and maintained schools and, indeed, the Cathedral Music Outreach project brings together children from a wide variety of backgrounds and cultures to make music together.

At the heart of our school is the aim to be an inclusive community where all are respected and all are valued. This finds a voice in the way that the spirituality of the school is manifested; liturgically in the Eucharist and informally through daily acts of collective worship. Song and silence have equal importance and the children help the adults who teach them to pray together.

For more than 850 years the Cathedral School has been a home for the Cathedral choristers who provide music for the daily services in the Cathedral during the singing term. Since 1994 girls have been admitted to the choir and are equal in status to the boy choristers originally founded by St Edward the Confessor in 1050. Over many years the Cathedral School has grown and is no longer simply a choir school. Academic excellence, a wide variety of subjects and achievement in sports as well as the performing arts are just as important as making music.

So our school is a community in the real sense of that word for it is bound up with the praying community of the Cathedral and with the boarding community including many choristers. In this regard it is unique and offers an education in which every aspect of the child is nurtured and in which giving something back to the wider community is encouraged.

2. Because the school is a Eucharistic Community it was easy to see how belonging to the Woodard family would help us with our aims and objectives; Exeter Cathedral School is not a school for the elite. It *is* a school where excellence is strived for but not at the cost of children who have special needs. All are valued and all have a voice; the Cathedral School looks beyond itself and, because the Dean and Chapter as Governors believe in the Woodard Vision, it was an easy step to take. We are thrilled that the Woodard family in Exeter has a maintained Comprehensive school as well as another independent school; this is the unique contribution of the Woodard family of schools to building bridges in education and practice.

3. Our fellowship with the Woodard family of schools allows us to discover new ways of being a community in our own situation. It allows us to meet and learn from others and this brings an added dimension to our school; we are not on our own, we belong to something greater. Our membership of the Woodard family of schools is very new but the ethos and values of our school are very old and we have something shared in common. To be a Eucharistic community means that our life is represented by sacrificial giving – a nourishing experience in which all, child and teacher, can reach their full potential and become more like Christ.

Head Boy: Arthur Prideaux

Hurstpierpoint College
West Sussex
Jeremy Sykes, Chaplain. Tim Manly, Head (Heather Beeby, Prep)

1. Hurstpierpoint College is a school of some 1,000 boys and girls from ages five to 18. A large number board on either a flexible, weekly or full basis from 13 with occasional boarding in the prep school.

The College has a strong religious ethos. It sees itself as a Christian community in which the Eucharist plays a focal part. At its weekly celebrations the College proclaims its values and the achievements of the children in equal measure.

Hurst offers an atmosphere in which pupils and staff enjoy strong relationships. These are based on a positive outlook, the desire to use one's energies to the utmost and a warmth which fosters a sense of security in its children. In this our pupils thrive knowing that they can take risks and in so doing learn rapidly in a mutually supportive environment.

The school tries to be inclusive in every sense whilst maintaining its distinctiveness. It looks to foster the best in every pupil and through its pastoral structure ensures that no one is overlooked. The achievements of the weaker members of the community are trumpeted as loudly as the stronger.

In this the school tries to play its part in contributing to the growth of the Kingdom of God here on Earth. It tries to be a community which prays, celebrates and proclaims that values of the Christian Gospel.

2. The College was founded in 1849 by Nathaniel Woodard and has always been a part of the Woodard family.

3. The Woodard ethos underpins all that the College tries to achieve. This ethos acts as a mainstay in the school's planning and thinking about the future. It helps us to be true to our calling and to keep us on the straight and narrow!

Head Boy: Joshua Hammond
Head Girl: Trixie Waggott

King's College and King's Hall School Taunton

Mark Smith, Chaplain. Richard Biggs, Head (King's College). Justin Chippendale, Head (King's Hall)

King's College, Taunton joined the Woodard family exactly 130 years ago. It was founded as King Alfred's College-School on 26 October 1880, the anniversary of the death of King Alfred. The roots of the school go back to Bishop Fox Grammar School in the town centre. This was founded in 1522 by the Bishop of Winchester, Richard Fox, a key figure in Henry VIII's Privy Council. Bishop Fox had a pelican at the heart of his crest and that powerful symbol of the parent bird drawing its own blood and taking its own life to feed its children remained with the school (by 1867 called Taunton College School) when it was moved from its site in Corporation Street to South Road in 1869. In 1879 the educational pioneer, Canon Nathaniel Woodard, bought the school and renamed it King's College.

A boys' school for 13 to 18-year-olds, King's College initially became co-educational in 1968 with the introduction of sixth-form girls. It is now a fully co-educational school. Today King's College is an Independent boarding school for boys and girls aged 14 to 18 and there are around 440 pupils.

Our all-ages houses are of tremendous benefit to all pupils and the curriculum remains unashamedly academic and traditional, with an emphasis on the demanding subjects which are still much valued by leading universities. These subjects are taught by experienced specialists.

Sixth-form pupils have the opportunity to complete the AQA Baccalaureate, which includes three A levels, an AS in Critical Thinking, an extended project and 100 hours of work experience, self-improvement and community service. We retain, in this way, the rigour, depth and flexibility of A levels while formally recognising the breadth of involvement of our pupils.

There are plenty of opportunities for our ambitious pupils to stretch their academic wings: classes are small and academic supervision is close and effective. There are speakers, visits, seminars, clubs and societies, debating, magazines; these allow pupils to go beyond mere exam preparation and to establish themselves as enthusiastic and skilful learners and scholars. We have established a tradition of taking sixth-form academic scholars on a trip to a European city in the Michaelmas Term.

The King's tutor system ensures close, personal support.

Many tours are arranged each year, including the sixth form biology trip to the Scilly Isles, sports tours, music trips, ski trips and language exchanges.

The wealth of extra-curricular opportunities for which this school is renowned ensures that pupils enjoy a well-rounded and fulfilling career. They are invariably incredibly busy and involved and, again, this experience is excellent preparation for life beyond school. We make sure that as far as possible activities do not clash and that it is possible for our pupils to do, for example, *both* music and sport to a high level.

Sixth formers enjoy freedoms and responsibilities not afforded to their younger brethren. There is a growing expectation that they play a meaningful role in setting standards and in helping with the running of the school. In return they express greater individuality in the way they dress and in the way they use their time.

We offer formal training in leadership as well as in confidence-building activities, learning skills seminars and 'soft skills' training.

Both boarders and day pupils benefit from their attachment to a boarding house: a home away from home, where they can meet others socially, store their books and kit and work at their own desk, surrounded by their own stuff.

In accordance with the Woodard ethos, the chapel is increasingly central to school life with a weekly Eucharist for the whole school community and other creative opportunities to worship. King's truly believes, as our founder did, that the spiritual component of education, with the Eucharist at the centre, is vital in the development of the whole person.

Our community is diverse, consisting of individuals of Faith as well as those of no Faith. We encourage the school community to explore freely their understanding of themselves in the world through a rich programme of academic, cultural, sport and social endeavour. But the touchstone for all is human spirituality as embodied in Jesus Christ.

In a world where religion and its practices have often been discredited or misunderstood, we believe in the importance of religious literacy and offer our pupils opportunities to study and explore great faith traditions of the world in a formal academic way.

There are also devotional opportunities on Friday mornings as well as for Sunday worship. On Tuesdays there is a popular late night candlelit reflection in the chapel followed by hot chocolate and doughnuts. Pupils are invited to share the thoughts, insights, and questions that affect their lives individually and communally. The chaplain is, as Woodard required, always available to the whole community for counselling, advice, and for baptisms, weddings and funerals.

At various times throughout the year, the school community joins together with parents and others for wonderful and moving acts of worship such as Remembrance Sunday, Ash Wednesday, Carols and nine lessons, Confirmation, Sung Evensong and the Christmas morning family Eucharist.

King's Hall School was originally known as Pyrland Hall and joined the Woodard family when it was bought by King's College at a public auction in 1951 for £10,000. The following September the junior school moved in.

Today, King's Hall School shares a Chaplain with King's College and the Woodard ethos is actively promoted in every area of school life. There is regular celebration of the Eucharist, adapted for children, and new pupils are being admitted to Communion before Confirmation every year. The devotions twice a week are used primarily for teaching children the doctrines of the Christian Faith and to pray in a meaningful way. The Chaplain also teaches Religious Studies.

Head Boy: Henry Close (King's College), Sam Sprague (King's Hall School)
Head Girl: Hannah Cartwright (King's College), Morgan Tottle (King's Hall School)

KING'S SCHOOL, ROCHESTER
KENT
John Thackray, Chaplain. Ian Walker, Head

We have 1,400 years' experience of preparing young people for the modern world. Our school pre-dates even the magnificent Norman cathedral of Rochester, which serves as our chapel. Although not the senior Woodard School, we are the oldest.

The Christian ethos of the School encourages children to an awareness of their own spirituality and personal faith. In all three parts of the School each day commences with a corporate act of worship. The Head Master advises new pupils at the start of each year that the most important thing that the School does is to worship God.

Our unique approach is built on four solid and proven foundations. First, children absorb principles of moral behaviour and respect for others that will serve them all their life; these principles derive from our Christian tradition.

Secondly, we stretch our pupils intellectually from their youngest years and train them to think for themselves; this is the best possible route to a good university and a good degree. Soft subjects and easy grades benefit no-one.

Then we focus on the whole person. Small classes enable us to know our pupils; individual attention gets the best out of them; and the wide range of extra-curricular activities lets them test and develop their interests and talents, whatever these may be.

Lastly and crucially, we engage with members of the King's family. At King's Rochester, education is still a calling, not just a job. Pupils are people, not just faces in a crowd. Our teachers earn respect, rather than demand it; and this motivates pupils to do well for them.

We are a co-educational (three to 18) school of 750 pupils; there are two boarding houses.

At the beginning of the 21st century our school became an Associate of the Woodard Foundation because we recognise that we hold in common with Woodard a vision of the School as a Christian community rooted in the Eucharist.

It means that we are sustained in our living of the faith by the knowledge that we are part of a wider family.

Head Boy: Michael Fedosiuk
Head Girl: Riti Patel

The King's School

Tynemouth, Tyne and Wear

Christopher Clinch, Chaplain. Ed Wesson, Head

The King's School, Tynemouth had been in existence in various forms for around 100 years before it was brought into the Woodard family and indeed gained its present name. By the 1950s Tynemouth School (as it was then known) was struggling financially and its numbers were small. The School had looked for purchasers in vain but the then vicar of the parish church of Holy Saviour's, Tynemouth Priory, wrote to the future headmaster Malcolm Nicholson who was on the Chapter of the Woodard Corporation asking whether the Corporation could take over the school. The Northern Chapter of the Woodard Corporation had as its chairman Eric Milner-White, who was at that time Dean of York. He enthusiastically accepted the challenge and despite numerous difficulties he brought Tynemouth School into the Woodard family.

By bringing the first day school into the Woodard Corporation, Eric Milner-White recognised that it would bring a new richness and diversity to the Woodard family as well as changing the character of the school. There was no attempt to imitate the other Woodard schools for it was recognised that King's would be different in many ways yet they share the same essential values.

So what about the school some fifty years later? The King's School in 2011 has grown into a large institution with pupils from four to 18 coming from across the region to attend. What is it that attracts them, for there are many other fine schools in the region in both the independent and state sectors they could attend?

There is a real quality about the education at King's, which is not just about academic achievements (although it holds its own on that front). Neither is it just about the many opportunities for extra-curricular activities that exist (although these are well supported and enjoyed). The real quality can be seen in the pupils themselves. When children are shown around the school (when considering applying for a place) it is the nature of our pupils that make so many pupils come to King's. Nearly all positive about the experience of being at school; confident in speaking to others; supportive and respectful of each other.

Being a Woodard school means that these qualities are affirmed. The King's School is proud of its inheritance and independence (the Geordie blood flows strongly through its veins!). But it recognises that like a true family it shares simple but fundamental values built upon the teaching of Christ himself, where fairness, tolerance, generosity and love are behind the education we offer.

Head Girl: Nikki Robinson

The King's School

Wolverhampton

John Allin, Head

The King's School, Wolverhampton is a Voluntary Aided Church of England school very much in a multi cultural and multi faith setting where we truly believe in Excellence through Diversity.

As Specialist Visual Arts College, also designated as a Specialist Sports College with Science, we provide opportunities for academic, creative, sporting and personal development for all our students.

We are extremely proud that our recent National Society Statutory Inspection of Anglican Schools confirmed that we were outstanding in every category. It highlighted that our shared Christian values underpinned all that we do whilst ensuring that the celebration of the "multi-racial, multi-faith" culture of our school ensures that respect, inclusion & community cohesion are at the heart of all of our activities. In addition the inspection recognised that our Arts College status contributed very strongly to our creative, inspiring and challenging curriculum.

We care passionately about all we do and take pride in ensuring that the atmosphere around school is happy and co-operative. We know our students are our best ambassadors. They like and take pride in their school and we cultivate their feeling of working together.

We are currently undergoing a massive campus redesign and building programme as we are a sample school in Wolverhampton LA's BSF programme. By September 2012 we will have a new school site with state of the art ICT facilities and other facilities. These are exciting times for all those involved in the school and we look forward to meeting these new challenges.

LANCING COLLEGE
WEST SUSSEX
and LANCING COLLEGE PREPARATORY SCHOOL AT MOWDEN
HOVE, EAST SUSSEX
Richard Harrison, Chaplain. Jonathan Gillespie, Head. Alan Laurent, Lancing Prep Head

I write this as Chaplain of Lancing College in November 2010, a good month to write such a reflection, for it is the 'Month of the Holy Souls'. Christians are always asked to pray for the souls of the faithful departed: every Mass here ends with the prayer, 'May the divine assistance remain with us always and may the souls of the faithful departed rest in peace …' to which the choir always responds with great gusto '… and rise in glory!' November, however, has a special emphasis on praying in this way, so it is that at the beginning of the month we kept All Souls' Day: pupils and staff were asked to give the Chaplain names of those who have died who they would like to pray for and there is always a good response to this and these names are placed on the altar on All Souls' Day. This can be of great comfort for those who have suffered bereavement. Our worship is a source of inspiration, of challenge but also of comfort and mass is offered, with the attendance of representatives from a 'duty house', every day here in term time.

We also kept All Saints' Day as a day of celebration for the whole school (we keep this as a School Eucharist, which we do every week, when the whole school with our exceptional Choir comes to Chapel for the offering of the Mass) and this is a day when we give thanks for the witness of the saints. The Christian life is above all one of thanksgiving to God for what has been achieved in Jesus Christ, and for his opening of the gates of heaven for all of us. This year we had as our preacher the Reverend Wendy Dalrymple, the new Chaplain at the Sir Robert Woodard Academy, which reminds us of our link with this new Woodard initiative and the strong support that we give to this academy and the one at Littlehampton, too. Our worship and our witness to God's love in Christ should turn us to 'the world beyond', in every sense, including simply the world beyond our school gates at the bottom of the drive.

This also brings to mind the strong emphasis on teaching the Christian faith here, both in Chapel and in the classroom, where all pupils take the Short Course GCSE in Religious Studies at the end of their second year here. This is part of our attempt to teach our pupils how to live and to love in this world – and also that our school is not just to prepare pupils for this world, but also for the next! We do this in the context of respect and tolerance of those of other faiths who are here, and who choose to come here, as they and their parents would like to attend a place of clear faith, rather than one with none. It so happens that at this time we are also preparing for a 'Thanksgiving Service' for the life of Susannah Whitty, an outstanding and inspirational housemistress here, who was instrumental in bringing successful co-education to the school. Lancing now offers a superb education for girls as well as boys.

Lancing College Chapel has become a place where old boys and girls want to return to – for baptisms, weddings and for memorial services. The very building itself speaks of Nathanial Woodard's love of this, his first school, and is where his chantry chapel is and where he lies in rest: for this reason it will be the focus of the celebrations of 21 March 2011, the reason for this publication. The Chapel is an outstanding example of neo-Gothic architecture and cannot be missed by anyone who drives along the south coast road (the A27), and is open to visitors all year round. We are used by many other organisations and amongst them for the celebration so the Chrism Mass in Holy Week, when the entire diocese gathers with its Bishop for a renewal of priestly vows and the blessing of the oils used for the rites of the Church. The Chapel has a peculiar and distinctive witness to the Catholic faith, worship and identity of the Church of England, admired and commended by visiting preachers and enthusiastically supported by a team of pupil sacristans, who believe worship must be worthy of the majesty of God.

At Lancing, we hope our lives together reflect something of Woodard's original vision: our care and love for one another take place within the context of a worshipping and eucharistic community, where love of God is translated into love of others. Not for nothing is one version of our motto '*Qui diligit Deum diligat et fratrem suum*' or, in translation, 'Those who love God, should love each other also.'

We do this through things like the biennial trip to Malawi, which has been going on for over 20 years and where hospitals, orphanages and places of refuge are built with our support and help. We mark Lent every year with a term devoted to raising money for charity: each of the nine houses has a week allocated to it and chooses which charity to support, on average raising at least £1,000 each. We have outreach, connecting the school with local communities in need, like primary schools, old peoples' homes and those who are handicapped, who find therapy in visiting the school farm.

This vision of the Woodard life in practice at Lancing can be summed up in the words which end the school prospectus:

> Young men and women leaving Lancing College take with them friendships, self-knowledge, tolerance, compassion, integrity, confidence built on achievement and a love of learning and adventure. They are unlikely ever again to have so many different things to do, so easily, or so many friends to share them with, but they will be equipped with essential skills and timeless values which will stay with them for the rest of their lives.

Head Boy: Benedict Pope
Head Girl: Libby Wright
Head Girl: Charlotte Blanden (Lancing Prep)

The Littlehampton Academy
Littlehampton, West Sussex
Paul Sanderson, Chaplain. Steve Jewell, Head

1. The Littlehampton Academy has been a Woodard school since September 2009. We have 1,700 students on role, including approximately 200 in our post-16 College. Our specialisms are Business & Enterprise and English. As the only secondary school in the seaside town of Littlehampton we draw students from some of the most deprived parts of West Sussex. Our creative and friendly students are developing a passion for understanding education in some of the world's poorest nations. In the past 18 months more than 60 students have volunteered in countries including Thailand, Ethiopia, Kenya, Sri Lanka and India. This is part of our mission to understand and then speak out about poverty and injustice in the world.

2. The governors of the predecessor school explored academy status as a way of gaining a building that was fit for purpose. The County Council investigated becoming co-sponsor, with Woodard taking the lead. Many meetings later we had a new name, a new uniform, a new principal and the very new role of Chaplain. These changes have had a huge impact on both the school and community at large.

3. Visitors to TLA comment on the warm and welcoming atmosphere and how smart our students look. We are organised in Chapters (schools within schools) to ensure we know and nurture all our students. Looking back at an historical hero, Nathaniel Woodard, gives our community the opportunity to learn and be inspired for the future. 2012 does not just mean the Olympics to Littlehampton because in September of that special year we will proudly walk into our new main building which will be a creative mixture of quality, practicality and inspiration. Thanks to Woodard, students at TLA now explore Christian beliefs and values, inclusively and creatively. Being a part of the Woodard family is increasing the hope, expanding the faith and drawing people together in our school, in our community and in our world.

Head Boy: Andy Sula
Head Girl: Emma Johnson

The Peterborough School
Peterborough, Cambridgeshire
Tim Whitwhell, Chaplain. Adrian Meadows, Head

1. Considerable energy and dedication among staff and pupils continuing to make remarkable progress as a vibrant School where the Woodard ethos daily reminds the community to discover their worth and vocation before God.

    Family atmosphere where the dynamism of a sure academic rigour co-exists with a gentle and humble presence that is focused but not pretentious.

    Burgeoning roll in pupil numbers where each child grows in confidence and self-esteem.

    Friendly and happy atmosphere where time is taken to care for one another and to value each person.

    School's particular strength: appreciation of creative expression: drama and music.

    Wide range of activities beyond classroom which is being supported by the new build in 2011 of a Sports Hall.

    Links with the wider community.

High academic success – small classes – outstanding classroom experience.

An environment where daily opportunities for maturity of heart and mind are afforded and individuals are encouraged to be themselves and to reach their full potential.

Education of Cathedral Probationers and Choristers. The link with the Cathedral is good.

Community where all are cherished, inspired and supported to become the people they are called to be.

24 September 2010 official name changed to The Peterborough School to reflect the incorporation of boys into the Senior School.

The Peterborough School is an independent school with nursery for boys and girls from six weeks to 18 years.

2.   School was incorporated into the Woodard family on 2 September 1974.

3.   The Woodard Corporation's ethos of faith, unity and vision is revealed most especially in the life and witness of the Chapel where all Senior School pupils attend Mass once a week, whilst pupils in the Preparatory Department attend a Service once a week in Chapel and Junior Mass once each half-term.

The Chapel of St Hugh of Lincoln and the ministry of the Chaplain remind the whole School community that The Peterborough School is a Woodard school where the Christian faith and quests of spirituality are of essential significance in the journey of education.

The Chapel and Chaplain remain at the heart of the School with the compassion and instruction of Christ pervading all that they are and do.

Since 1979 there have been nine full-time Chaplains.

Head Girl: Katie Avison

Prestfelde School
Gareth Parry, Chaplain. Philip Banks, Acting Head.

Prestfelde School is a 'free-standing', co-educational, preparatory school for pupils aged three to 13. It was established in 1929 and only became a member of the Woodard Corporation in 1949. The first Headmaster was the Reverend G.K. Dovey (1929-49). The administrative block, the Dovey Centre is named after him.

The present Headmaster is Mr Mark Groome who took up the post in September 2007. There are currently just under 300 pupils on roll. Many Prestfelde pupils go on to very prestigious senior schools: Shrewsbury, Moreton Hall, Adams' Grammar School, Wrekin College, Oswestry and many others.

The Chapel at Prestfelde does not have the architectural merit of Lancing Chapel. It is a simple wooden structure, built in the 1960s and dedicated to St Alban, a saint who had associations in the locality of Prestfelde. There has been an effort made in recent years to restore the Anglo-Catholic ethos of Woodard in Prestfelde Chapel. There is a weekly voluntary Eucharist held every Wednesday break, to which a group of faithful boys come. A whole-school Eucharist has been established and is celebrated five times each term, on Red-Letter days, such as the Epiphany, the Presentation, Ash Wednesday and Saints' Days.

We have been very encouraged by the positive response of our pupils to the sacramental life of the Chapel. We have reinstated the role of Chapel Wardens and Sacristan in the last year. In each whole-school celebration, we have a crucifer, acolytes and servers and all are very eager to take part in reading or leading the intercessions.

The number of Confirmation candidates has been very healthy. Last May, ten boys and one mother were confirmed by the Bishop of Shrewsbury, the Right Reverend Mark Rylands.

This year six boys will be confirmed on 3 March, again by the Bishop of Shrewsbury.

We hope to build on this good record and continue to promote the Christian ethos of the school and the centrality of the Eucharist to the life of the community.

The Chapel Team this year are: Wardens – Tommy Dodd and Oliver Pope; Sacristan – Matthew Chakraverty; Assistant – Scott Reynolds.

The Head Boy is Jack Bywater and the Head Girl is Georgia Huddleston. Both are delightful pupils and carry out their duties professionally and cheerfully.

The Chaplain, Father Gareth Parry has been at Prestfelde for the last two years. He was received as a Companion of the Society of St Francis in the school Chapel on 10 May 2010.

Prestfelde is a co-educational, three to 13 Independent Preparatory School. As a proud member of the Woodard family of schools, it is committed to educating children within a Christian community. The School aims to provide a stimulating academic, spiritual and physical environment in which boys and girls can develop their own talents and grow in confidence.

Prestfelde pupils care for each other and support each other. Girls and boys grow to know and understand each other. Forged here are friendships which last for years. Above all, Prestfeldians have a zest for life and for fun.

Its beautiful 30-acre site is home to a purpose-built Senior School (ages 10-13) and Middle School (ages seven to nine) as well as a Pre Prep school, called Little Prestfelde (ages three to seven). Many facilities are shared between the three departments. These include superb modern facilities for Music, Art and Design/Technology, an indoor swimming pool, tennis and netball courts and sports hall.

Prestfelde House includes the boarding house, the medical centre, Headmaster's Study and the main school office: the adjacent Lambart Hall is the school's dining hall. The extensive grounds provide for a full range of sports and outdoor activities within a secure setting. There is a golf course and an adventure playground for the younger children.

Head Boy: Jack Bywater
Head Girl: Georgina Huddleston

Queen Mary's School
Thirsk, North Yorkshire
John Payne, Chaplain. Robert McKenzie Johnston, Head

Queen Mary's School was formed originally in 1925 by the Woodard Corporation as a Prep School for Queen Margaret's at Escrick (near York), then a Woodard senior girls' school. The School was originally based at Duncombe Park in Helmsley, the home of Lord Feversham, and was known then as 'Duncombe Park School'. Queen Mary later invited the School to rename itself after her, and so it became gradually known as Queen Mary's. In 1985 Lord Feversham asked for his house back, so the School moved to new premises at Baldersby Park, another Palladian house, near Thirsk.

Queen Mary's was originally a full boarding girls' prep school. Over the years it introduced a senior school (up to 16) and, on moving to Baldersby Park, began to take weekly boarders and day girls. It also introduced a small pre-prep department, with both boys and girls.

Today Queen Mary's is a non-selective day and boarding school for girls up to the age of 16. The boarders are mostly weekly boarders, some of whom choose to stay at school over the weekend. As with all Woodard schools, the Christian faith lies at the heart of the School's ethos and character. Most of the girls are Church of England, but the School has a small and active Roman Catholic community of both girls and staff, and both branches of the Church share each others' services and worship. As a North Yorkshire school it has yet to encounter the multi-cultural and multi-faith challenges and opportunities to be found elsewhere in Britain.

Queen Mary's has been a Woodard school all its life. The ethos of a Woodard school is to be found everywhere, particularly in its emphasis on a worshipping Eucharistic community, and on its acceptance of each and every child as a human being first, one loved by God and not to be judged by the character and abilities God has given to her. The challenge of remaining a small but viable non-selective school which nurtures each child in a loving community, encouraging the able to flourish while each child achieves all that she is capable of, remains at the heart of Queen Mary's mission.

Head Girl: Alice Barker

RANBY HOUSE SCHOOL
RETFORD, NOTTINGHAMSHIRE
Darren Moore, Chaplain. David Sibson, Head

Ranby House School is currently a three to 13 co-educational preparatory school just off the A1 between the towns of Worksop and Retford. The main building has some history and was apparently owned by a retired military man before being bought by the school in the late 1940s. One of the dorms has lots of lovely 'Mousey' Thompson panelling and is known as 'Mouse' dorm to this day and is loved by those in the junior end of the school who find themselves there often boarding for the first time.

We are indeed a boarding school and whilst this year has seen our boarding numbers decline considerably there has certainly been a long and glorious tradition of boarding at Ranby House. We have the older and more traditional (and just possibly a little more drafty!) boys' house looked after by Mr and Mrs Pymm. Then there is the more modern girls' house looked after by Mr and Mrs Searle.

There was a time when Ranby House did not exist in its own right but was in fact on the Worksop College site. At some point the College needed the space for another boarding house and so it was that Ranby House forged out on its own a bit, though the links between the two schools remain very strong and a very large number of our Year 8 students do continue their senior education at Worksop College.

The Woodard side of life here is extremely important. The Chapel could be said to be at the very centre of our life here. The newly refurbished space is the setting throughout the year where we punctuate our terms with the feasts and festivals of the Christian year. The autumn term and new school year sees us in a spirit of thanksgiving for our Harvest Festival through to Remembrance and there then follows a whole host of Advent and Christmas events. Then there is Ash Wednesday in the spring term, a term which ends with our palm procession from the performing arts centre to the Chapel. The summer term begins with a special Easter service where we bless our Paschal candle and the end of the term sees us bid our leavers farewell as we wish them God speed and God bless at a special Eucharistic celebration. The Eucharist is an important part of life here at Ranby and it has been a blessing to share it with so many parents, visitors and friends on a Saturday morning.

Head Boy: Jake Turner
Head Girl: Emily Mitchell

SAINT GEORGE'S CHURCH OF ENGLAND SCHOOL
GRAVESEND, KENT
Anne Southgate, Headteacher

Saint George's is a co-educational high school in a selective education authority. We are a Humanities College, with the mission statement, 'All Different, All Equal'. We believe firmly in valuing the talents of all of our students and promote an understanding of cultural diversity. As a school with a Church of England foundation, we see ourselves as a Christian school, rather than a school for Christians, in that we serve the multi-cultural and multi-faith community in which we live. In this we believe we are following Jesus' example of service and compassion.

The School became involved with Woodard in the 1990s when it was seeking to emphasise its distinctive nature as a Church school.

Being associated with Woodard today serves to remind us of the Christian principles underpinning our mission and allows us to feel part of a greater body of schools who also seek to be Christian schools.

Head Boy: Mark Singer
Head Girl: Rachel Shoard

ST JAMES' SCHOOL
GRIMSBY
Sue Isaac, Head

The School was founded in 1880 as the choir school of St James' Parish Church and it still serves this function today. It became a fully incorporated member of the Woodard family in 1969. Independent, it has 240 boys and girls, aged two and a half to 18, including 40 boarders.

Head Boy: Enoch Wong
Head Girl: Marianne Kempe

ST MARGARET'S SCHOOL
EXETER
Jane Frost, Lay Chaplain. Sheila Cooper, Head

Friendly, caring, academically rigorous, community minded, outward looking: these attributes give St Margaret's School in Exeter its distinct identity. The family atmosphere is also a marked feature of daily life at this unique and quirky (in the best way) Woodard school. It's a school where individuals are truly valued. Over the years, St Margaret's has broadened its provision and currently it offers a rounded education to pupils between the ages of three and 18. The Senior Department remains single sex and we have one of the few all girls' CCF contingents in the country.

Founded in 1902, and housed in Georgian buildings, the School could be described as a grand old lady or a feisty young woman! There is a strong sense of continuity about it as the values which underpinned its foundation – the importance of the individual, helping others, aspiring to excellence in everything, fostering a sense of service and responsibility, communicating enthusiasm for life – continue to be apparent today. Over the years, however, extra-curricular provision has grown. Senior School students benefit from language exchanges and being part of the Comenius projects which have caused us to forge links with schools in Belgium, Denmark and Poland among others. Opportunities to visit India crop up biennially as we take a particular interest in the charity which supports the Goodwill Village there. The confidence of students is also nurtured through the Duke of Edinburgh Award Scheme. In the last 10 years, we have achieved more than 100 gold awards. Taking part in the Ten Tors challenge is also an annual tradition and contributes further to our 'can do' ethos.

Music and Drama have long been particular strengths of the curriculum and concerts and productions involving all ages continue to provide highlights in the calendar whether it's four of the School's choral groups contributing to the St Margaret's Day Eucharist in the Cathedral, the elite Chapel Choir singing at Cathedral Evensong, a lively dramatic presentation of the 'Lion King' story, or a fizzy wizzy Musical Theatre taster Saturday.

The Woodard link dates back to 1968 when the redoubtable and much loved Miss Morford took the School into a larger Christian community. Where is our Christian Ethos apparent? Inspection reports and parental comment pinpoint its existence in the pastoral care, in the warm relationships between staff and students, in vertically grouped activities, in Christian Unions and prayer meetings involving staff, parents and students. Whole school and key stage assemblies and Eucharists capitalise on the faith experiences of visiting speakers and insights from our home grown team! Confirmation and Admission to Communion are offered annually. Fund-raising projects such as the Mustard Seed Relief Missions' Christmas Shoe Box appeal are enthusiastically supported. So all in all, I would hope our leavers have experienced something of 'life in all its fullness'.

Head Girl: Lucy Norman-Walker

St Mary's Preparatory School
Lincoln
Edward Bowes-Smith, Chaplain. Andrew Salmond Smith, Head

St Mary's Preparatory School was established in 1950 by a group of local business professionals who felt that the city of Lincoln lacked the sort of school to which they would want to send their own children.

The School is based within a Grade I listed building in Pottergate, adjacent to the Cathedral and within the historic core of Lincoln. Step inside St Mary's walls and you enter one of the city's great secret gardens which provide a secure environment for the nursery, pre-prep and prep pupils.

In 2010 St Mary's celebrated its diamond jubilee. Over the years substantial development has taken place. Purpose built classrooms, administrative offices and an octagonal, purpose-built hall were completed in 1995. This was followed by the opening in 1999 of a £250,000 purpose-built Early Years Centre, a new flood-lit Astroturf in 2001.

A proudly independent school, the Board of Governors became increasingly conscious that in order to maintain standards and continued success, staff development was of vital significance. It was becoming increasingly challenging for 'stand alone' prep schools to deliver quality professional development and it was for this reason the Board decided to associate with the Woodard group of schools.

The School has always had a Christian ethos which the association with Woodard has helped to strengthen. The appointment of a chaplain and the greater opportunities for worship in the School, the Cathedral and the parish church are bringing a new rhythm to the life of the School.

Head Boy: Sam Jones
Head Girl: Elfie Cracroft-Eley

St Michael and All Angels Church of England Academy

Camberwell, London

Liz Oglesby, Chaplain. Colin Boxall, Head

The School was founded in 1661, with the current school building on Wyndham Road, Camberwell, first known as Archbishop Michael Ramsey School, founded in 1972. The Archbishop, Michael Ramsey himself laid the foundation stone for the new building on 4 November 1972. The new Academy, St Michael and All Angels Church of England Academy with specialisms in Science and Health, opened in 2007, and remains a dynamic educational opportunity for all who are educated here. Although the name and the site of the school has changed several times since it was originally founded in 1661, its Church of England heritage, tradition and spirituality continue to thrive and flourish. With the Parish Church of St Michael and All Angels sharing the site, we are blessed with the Academy and the local Church working much closer together over the past five years or so. This is due in part to the Vicar of the parish serving the Academy as Chaplain, and also the partnership work that has gone into designing a new Academy build, which will include a new distinctive but connected Parish Church building.

Our affiliation to Woodard continues through the many changes we have been through, and onwards, as we look forward to our future. Our Executive Headteacher, our Chaplain and a number of our Governors (who are Woodard Fellows), maintain the contact and benefit from the support and ethos of the Woodard family. As we look forward to the regeneration of our buildings, and continue to work hard to raise the standards of excellence in our Academy, we will continue to look to all our wider connections, including the Woodard family, for prayer, support and fellowship in times of continuing challenge and opportunity, that lie ahead of us at the Academy.

Our Academy prayer:
O magnificent Father,
we thank you for allowing us to have this moment in time with you.
We pray that our Academy will forever prosper in your name.
Empower us in every way whilst we are at the Academy today.
Bless our footsteps
and lead us into your truth,
from now until all eternity,
through Jesus Christ our Lord.
Amen.

Head Boy: Wale Shekete
Head Girl: Ivy Dei Kotey

St Olave's Grammar School
Orpington, Kent
Andrew McClellan, Chaplain. Aydin Önaç, Head

St Olave's Grammar School first appeared, as an Affiliated School, in the 1999 Woodard Kalendar.

Some 18 months earlier Jack Newby, Chairman of Governors and Tony Jarvis, Headmaster had hosted a visit to the School by Bishop Michael Adie. Bishop Michael had become Provost of the old Southern Division of Woodard Schools, having previously been Bishop of Guildford and the Education Spokesman for the Church of England in the House of Lords. His vision was to extend and enrich the Woodard Mission by bringing into its number a mix of State schools from very different environments and circumstances. The common factor was that all the schools had the Anglican Faith at the heart of their communities. Bishop Adie was ahead of his time, anticipating the subsequent developments and promotion of State and independent school partnerships. The School Governors and Foundation approved acceptance of the invitation. The benefits for St Olave's have been considerable and quietly influential. The Heads, Chaplains and Heads of Religious Education Departments have regular meetings and conferences which have provided information and inspiration. The students through the Woodard Prefects Training Courses and the Oxbridge Master Classes have similarly been enthused and made new friends from all backgrounds across the country. The most significant impact on the St Olave's School came through our partnership with Hurstpierpoint College and the exchange of our Pupil Tracking System with their Learning Zone Website. The staff involved travelled between the schools to see and learn and in the process helped both institutions to take their own programmes to an even higher level. Over a decade on a key element of the plan for the future in Woodard is to have clusters of schools working together and exchanging best practice within the context of our Anglican foundations. St Olave's we hope will play its part in that new development.

Head Boy: Harry McAleer

St Peter's CE (A)
Exeter
Mark Perry, Head

St Peter's CE (A) High School and International
Language College
Stoke on Trent
Maria Rubin, Chaplaincy Team. Bryan Carr, Head

St Peter's C of E (Aided) High School and International Language College is a high achieving over-subscribed 11 to 16 mixed comprehensive school. We strive to serve our young people by setting the highest standards of teaching and learning and community life thus enabling everyone to grow in God's love, wisdom and strength.

We aim to foster an enjoyment of learning by providing an excellent education based on Christian beliefs and values as well as encouraging students to develop their full God-given potential, ensuring they experience Christian worship and life, giving them a sound basis for their own life choices and helping them learn that it is better to serve than to be served. At St Peter's all are known, nurtured, challenged and loved.

Worship occupies a central place in our school community. We celebrate the Eucharist collectively inviting all students, staff, Governors and parents/carers to participate. Our worship team, orchestra and choir also contribute significantly to collective praise and worship and we encourage as many students as possible to take an active role during the service.

We continue to introduce other forms of more contemporary worship events which have proved to be very popular with the students and staff. We have noticed that all who participate become more confident in expressing their faith openly amongst their peers.

Recently we have developed the use of a multi-faith Prayer Room which the students have renamed as the 'Spiritual Window'. This has contributed significantly in encouraging the students to use the room uninhibitedly for prayer. The views of students are regularly sought and this led to our recent 'Zahraa's Day' where students led prayers and raised money to support one of our Year 10 students who is critically ill in hospital. The School is full of happy faces, acts of kindness, support, forgiveness and charitable acts. For example a number of students recently took the lead, by delivering an assembly to the whole school, in raising money to support victims in Pakistan. We continue to support numerous charities throughout the year and have just started our shoe box appeal 'Operation Christmas Child' to send out to children in need at Christmas time.

As a community we uphold the values of Nathaniel Woodard and as a Woodard School feel supported working towards Faith, Unity and Vision. It is comforting to know that other Woodard schools are praying for us at St Peter's. Being part of the Woodard family adds a wider spiritual dimension to our school community as seen in our RE department developing the Face to Faith project supported by Woodard. We also gain strength from feeling that we are part of a larger family and not alone in our walk with God.

Head Boy: Tom Brazier
Head Girl: Grace Mahony

S PETER'S COLLEGIATE SCHOOL
WOLVERHAMPTON
Adrian Richards, Acting Principal

1. The mission of S Peter's Collegiate School, rooted in our common life as a worshipping Christian community, is to educate the whole person so that everyone may find the keys to become all that God has uniquely put it within them to be. The right of every child to the best education possible underpins all we do at the school. We strive to be a very good comprehensive school responding to continuing change in education and society. We openly accept the challenge of blending well tried and tested, and indeed very successful teaching and learning methods, with innovative and exciting strategies for the future. We offer our students the best opportunities and facilities to support their learning needs. We want students to develop and mature as individuals. To do this requires compliance with some very basic and common sense rules that allow for the whole school community to thrive. We are not afraid to declare our belief in values such as honesty, tolerance and respect and to talk about them openly within the context of the Christian Gospel.

Equally, school should be an enjoyable and stimulating experience for all, and we all have responsibilities to ensure that this is the case – students and staff alike.

2. S Peter's Collegiate School became affiliated to the Woodard family in 1991. Basically, the School promoted a similar vision and ethos, where the education on offer was open to all and the Eucharist was at the heart of its Worship and spiritual life. It was clear that much could be shared with the Woodard family. The Senior Provost was a frequent visitor to the School – each term in fact and also presided at some of our Eucharists. The Head of Religious Studies and the Chaplain have made significant contributions to educational and spiritual projects organised by Woodard and the last two Principals – the Reverend Huw Bishop and his predecessor Mr Peter Crook are Fellows of the Woodard Corporation. Musicians and choristers from S Peter's have willingly joined with students from other Woodard schools in local and national celebrations – notably at the Royal Albert Hall, Symphony Hall in Birmingham and Stoke on Trent. Our Head Boy and Head Girl and other Senior Prefects take part in the annual Senior Prefects conference and various staff have contributed towards revision courses for A Level students.

3. S Peter's Collegiate School promotes its Woodard identity both locally and nationally. It proclaims and celebrates this through its literature, its worship and in its dealings with parents. Being part of a larger organisation gives particular credence to the School as an arm of mission within the Church – and the School's current heavy oversubscription for places is evidence that such an education is popular with families. This is particularly significant for S Peter's as a nationally acclaimed 'Leading Edge' school working in such close partnership with schools in differing circumstances and contexts. S Peter's is now directly involved in Woodard's exciting and innovative work with academy development, and particularly so with the proposed St Peter's Academy in Stoke on Trent in partnership with the Diocese of Lichfield.

Head Boy: George Stuart
Head Girl: Rosie O'Donnell

St Saviour's and St Olave's Church of England School

Southwark, London

Kes Grant, Chaplain. Irene Bishop, Head

St Saviour's and St Olave's School has a rich history dating back to 1562 when it received a charter from Queen Elizabeth I for the 'younglings' of the area. Its current site was opened in 1903. It is a Church of England comprehensive secondary school for girls in the multi-cultural and vibrant London Borough of Southwark.

The School became affiliated to Woodard when our current head Dr Irene Bishop made the links in 2002.

Woodard schools are distinctive because they all have the Eucharist as central to their worshipping life. This School has a faithful tradition of monthly lunchtime Eucharists that are attended voluntarily as well as annual whole year Eucharists. Although that is very important to us, in this school, what makes us unique is that we live out our dismissal from the Eucharist. Everyday, staff and students 'love and serve the Lord' as they go about regular activities. We care about each other and show each other the compassionate face of God. All our students are taught about 'agape' and that this school will love all of them not just their ability to perform academically.

Another aspect of Woodard life this School appreciates and gains benefit from are the separate annual conferences for heads and chaplains. both the head teacher and chaplain come back from these events enriched by the fellowship and networking of colleagues from very different perspectives and contexts.

The students also benefit from the Senior Prefect training and the Master Classes. For our girls this is an opportunity to meet other students who may be coming from a rural context as well as a great opportunity for students to meet and exchange experiences from the Independent Sector as well as State Schools.

Our open Christian tradition at St Saviour's and St Olave's is extremely important to us and we offer spiritual care to people of all faiths and none, whether they are students, parents/carers, teachers, support staff or Governors. The best way of explaining this is the way so many people from all traditions and none come to our annual All Souls' Service. This is a service where people can remember someone who has died who touched and enriched their lives. Candles are lit in honour of those who have died and messages are placed on the remembrance tree. All are welcome and all are comfortable and held securely by our Christian tradition whatever background they are coming from.

We are proud of the young people coming in nervously at Year 7, who leave school as confident and caring young women because of the whole package of teaching and care, challenge and support they get from us that is rooted and embodied in our Christian ethos and tradition.

Head Girl: Victoria Sylver

The Sir Robert Woodard Academy
Lancing, West Sussex
Carole Bailey, Head

Smallwood Manor
Uttoxeter, Staffordshire
Mike Harrison, Head

1. Smallwood retains the small, family atmosphere which has characterised it for many decades. The School has been through a process of evolution; from being a boys only boarding school with a 13+ transfer, Smallwood has now become a co-educational day school with children leaving us at the end of Year 6 (11+). It has its own self-contained Pre-Preparatory Department which opened in 1984 and, as part of its evolution, Smallwood opened a term-time only Nursery 1989 and in September 2006 the Nursery changed to being open all-year round, Monday to Friday 8.00 a.m. to 6.00 p.m. Despite those changes, that sense of belonging to a small school family which cares for each child remains and that sense of fun, sharing and learning together that characterises each family continues to be true of the Smallwood family.

2. Smallwood began its life at Denstone College, a fellow Woodard school, in 1902 and has been a member of the Woodard Corporation ever since, even though the School moved to its present site in the 1930s.

3. Being a Woodard-owned school means a great deal to Smallwood. The Christian faith that inspired Nathaniel Woodard continues to pervade all the school stands for and informs all the school does and aspires to. The way that the children are educated is based upon the sincere Christian belief that every human being, the pinnacle of God's wonderful creation, is highly precious and should be valued and respected; this includes oneself.

   Sharing those values and seeking to spread that influence further afield is both challenging and exciting. The Woodard family has grown as that vision finds fulfilment in more and more areas of the country. The desire to build a Woodard school in Kenya sees this vision growing into the next phase and will be tangible and visible evidence of the charitable motivation to carry the Woodard ethos abroad. As we celebrate the 200th anniversary of Nathaniel Woodard, I can think of no better way of marking this special anniversary year – a lasting, living and meaningful memorial to his vision.

St Wilfrid's COFE High School and Technology College
Blackburn
David Whyte, Headmaster

1. St Wilfrid's is a voluntary aided 11 to 18 High School and Technology College that serves the Blackburn Diocese. It has a robust and challenging Mission Statement and the school ethos is graded as outstanding by OFSTED.

   The gospel is at the forefront of our teaching and worship and, in recent years, especially within the Sixth Form, we are catering for other faiths within this distinctly Christian school. This reflects the development and growth of Blackburn as a town within the Diocese.

2. Whilst the former Bishop of Blackburn, the Right Reverend Alan Chesters, was representing the Church in the Lords, he encouraged my predecessor, Linda Robinson, to become affiliated with the Woodard family. As we have the Gospel and Eucharist at the centre of our worship it was felt that being part of the Woodard family enhanced and helped develop this Christian focus.

3. Affiliation with the Woodard family enables staff, students and governors to be part of a national focus on church education. The attendance at conferences for heads, chaplains and other leaders within the school is central to us reviewing our ethos and our Christian character. The students have benefited tremendously from master classes, prefects conferences, singing in Birmingham with the Woodard Choir and preparing for similar celebrations related to Nathaniel Woodard's 200th anniversary.

Head Boy: Alex Ashcroft
Head Girl: Jessica Hines

Trinity School
Belvedere, Kent
Ian Collins, Head

Trinity School is a well established and successful Church of England Diocesan comprehensive school in the Diocese of Rochester and the London Borough of Bexley. The

Christian spiritual ethos is at the heart of the everyday organisation of the School. Every child attends a daily Act of Worship and regular Eucharists are celebrated by our chaplain and local clergy.

We maintain high standards of behaviour and discipline throughout the school and visitors regularly comment on the calm and ordered atmosphere that they encounter. Our children say that they love their school and feel safe.

As part of an Excellence Improvement Partnership and as a Specialist College for the Arts and Humanities we have established successful and productive links and partnerships with other schools and the local community.

We are proud to be affiliated to the Woodard schools, a link which arose from our association with St George's School in Gravesend, another Church of England school in the Rochester Diocese. Our link with Woodard helps to underline and promote the Christian ethos which is paramount in all that we do.

Head Boy: Priyal Raja
Head Girl: Harriette Dowsett

WORKSOP COLLEGE

WORKSOP, NOTTINGHAMSHIRE

Paul Finlinson, Chaplain. Roy Collard, Head

Worksop College was founded in 1890, the last school to be founded by Canon Woodard himself before his death in 1891. Sadly Woodard did not live to see the College open in 1895.

Today we are a co-educational independent school, standing on the edge of Clumber Park in Nottinghamshire, with more than 400 pupils aged 13 to 18. Over half of the pupils are boarders, some full, some weekly, and some 'flexi'.

The School offers a traditional education, with classroom and boarding facilities grouped around a typical Woodard quadrangle. Recent investment includes the opening of a second Astroturf, a brand-new girls' boarding house, a sports hall with a climbing wall, refurbished science laboratories and two Food and Nutrition classrooms.

The College is a Woodard Incorporated School and this status underpins the nature of the school today. The centre of the life of the College is the Chapel, dedicated to St Cuthbert, and opened in 1911. Our Chapel centenary, therefore, coincides with Woodard's bicentenary. The Eucharist on Friday mornings, with a setting by the choir, is the high point of the College's week, giving the whole school an opportunity for worship and reflection. Voluntary services on Saints' Days and occasional discussion groups enhance the Woodard Christian experience. The houses are proud to support the community beyond the school through charitable giving.

2011 is a special year for Worksop College, proudly celebrating Woodard's bicentenary and our own Chapel centenary. To mark the latter there will be a Flower Festival in May and a Centenary Service on 6 October.

Thanks be to God.

Head Boy: William Woods
Head Girl: Sophie Clay

Index